There are plenty of books on
for those firmly established in the p............. .... _ ....
primer for those considering or just commencing this marvelous and complex
work. Readers will find this book to be clear and practical.

—Brent Peery, DMin
Director of Chaplaincy Services
Memorial Hermann, Texas Medical Center, Houston, Texas

At last, here is an absolutely practical book that is filled with valuable and worthwhile information for all chaplains of all disciplines. In *Essential Chaplain Skill Sets,* Dr. Keith Evans draws upon his vast academic knowledge, and his network of other skilled chaplains and personal experience to present a book that should become required reading for all chaplains.

As a ten-year veteran of law enforcement chaplaincy, now serving in the most ethnically diverse county in the United States (Fort Bend County, Texas), I found the chapters on understanding spirituality and world faith expressions very insightful and beneficial. I also appreciate that Dr. Evans presents a variety of very useful models and assessment tools to discover the spiritual and/or religious needs of those we have the opportunity to interact with in our roles as chaplains. I highly recommend this book for all chaplains, and I intend to make it required reading for the association of local law enforcement chaplains I lead.

—Chaplain Clifton Cummings
Senior Chaplain with the International Conference of Police Chaplains
President of Fort Bend County First Responder Chaplains Association
Sugar Land, Texas

Where was this book when I was a clinical pastoral education student? This volume so ably introduces key components of public ministry and then puts those elements together in a way that gives potential pastoral caregivers an overview of the noble task of chaplaincy. The well-developed themes of chaplaincy fundamentals, religious faith expression, and spiritual appraisal would have been beneficial to me on my CPE journey some time ago, and it serves today as an effective reminder to me of the nobility of my calling.

The contributor's writing style suits an audience of like-minded individuals exploring a pastoral calling, and it will appeal to other professions in their understanding of pastoral care. As one who aspires to become a pastoral educator, I would recommend this volume to all my students.

—Chaplain Peter L. Ward, DMin
ACPE Supervisory Student and Clinical Chaplain
Banner Heath System, Phoenix, Arizona

After spending the last forty years in chaplaincy service, I have come to understand the value and importance of finely tuned knowledge, skills, and abilities within the profession of chaplaincy. Having experientially practiced military chaplaincy, law enforcement chaplaincy, and health care chaplaincy, I can unequivocally support and expound upon the importance of fully developed skill sets for chaplains. Keith Evans has done a masterful job in the publishing of this most important and foundational book, *Essential Chaplain Skill Sets,* as he expounds on the specific skills in the performance of caring for other in times of need and distress.

—Michael W. Langston, DMin
Captain, Chaplain Corps, US Navy (Ret.)
Author, *A Journey of Hope*
Professor of Chaplaincy
Columbia International University
Columbia, South Carolina

What you have with *Essential Chaplain Skill Sets* is a pastoral practitioner's guide to proven skills learned through compassionate care and competent practice. Keith is a pastoral clinician sharing out of his own experience and doing his part to assist his pastoral colleagues in congregational and clinical settings and building upon their own art of pastoral care. He is a pragmatic realist and a patient teacher. Thank you, Keith, for this good companion book for those of us on the journey of becoming better clinical pastors.

—Rev. Mark Hart, DMin, BCC
ACPE Supervisor
Director of Clinical Pastoral Education
Baptist Health System, San Antonio, Texas

ESSENTIAL CHAPLAIN *Skill Sets*

Discovering Effective Ways to Provide Excellent Spiritual Care

CHAPLAIN KEITH EVANS

WestBow Press
A DIVISION OF THOMAS NELSON
& ZONDERVAN

Copyright © 2017 Chaplain Keith Evans.

All rights reserved. No part of this book may be used or reproduced by any means, graphic, electronic, or mechanical, including photocopying, recording, taping or by any information storage retrieval system without the written permission of the author except in the case of brief quotations embodied in critical articles and reviews.

This book is a work of non-fiction. Unless otherwise noted, the author and the publisher make no explicit guarantees as to the accuracy of the information contained in this book and in some cases, names of people and places have been altered to protect their privacy.

Scripture quotations are from the ESV® Bible (The Holy Bible, English Standard Version®), copyright © 2001 by Crossway, a publishing ministry of Good News Publishers. Used by permission. All rights reserved.

Scripture taken from the New King James Version®. Copyright © 1982 by Thomas Nelson. Used by permission. All rights reserved.

WestBow Press books may be ordered through booksellers or by contacting:

WestBow Press
A Division of Thomas Nelson & Zondervan
1663 Liberty Drive
Bloomington, IN 47403
www.westbowpress.com
844-714-3454

Because of the dynamic nature of the Internet, any web addresses or links contained in this book may have changed since publication and may no longer be valid. The views expressed in this work are solely those of the author and do not necessarily reflect the views of the publisher, and the publisher hereby disclaims any responsibility for them.

Any people depicted in stock imagery provided by Thinkstock are models, and such images are being used for illustrative purposes only. Certain stock imagery © Thinkstock.

ISBN: 978-1-9736-0011-4 (sc)
ISBN: 978-1-9736-0012-1 (hc)
ISBN: 978-1-9736-0010-7 (e)

Library of Congress Control Number: 2017913209

Print information available on the last page.

WestBow Press rev. date: 8/24/2017

ACKNOWLEDGMENTS

I am indebted to several individuals who assisted me with their unique perspectives for several sections of this book. For chapter 6, I interviewed Rev. Leslie Kee, who assisted me with insights into the spiritual perspectives of humanism. I interviewed Dr. Devjit "Tom" Roy for chapters 7 and 8, and he served as a great adviser and counsel to me as I prepared the sections on Buddhism and Hinduism. I am also indebted to Chaplain Zac Buhuro who assisted me with chapter 13. Zac's cultural and ethnic diversity as well as his experience in hospice and end-of-life chaplaincy was highly beneficial for the discussion of spiritual needs assessments.

Rev. Leslie Kee, MDiv

Rev. Kee leads a Unitarian Universalist congregation. She has also served as a women's prison chaplain and works in hospice care. She describes herself as a religious humanist, an earth-based spiritualist and activist, feminist theologian, and life-long learner. Rev. Kee holds a bachelor of science degree from Colorado State University in Fort Collins, Colorado, and has an earned master of divinity degree from Meadville Lombard Theological School in Chicago, Illinois.

Devjit "Tom" Roy, MD

Dr. Roy is an internal hospitalist. He grew up in New Jersey within the Vedic (Braham) Hindu faith tradition. Dr. Roy has personally explored many areas of spirituality. He routinely addresses spirituality with his patients, and he sees the spiritual realm a critical part of holistic health care. Dr. Roy has a biomedical engineering degree from Rutgers School of Engineering and a medical degree from the American University of Antiqua's College of Medicine. Dr. Roy currently practices as a hospitalist at the Wyoming Medical Center in Casper, Wyoming.

Zacarias C Buhuro MA, MDiv, BCC

Chaplain Zac is a board-certified professional chaplain (National Association of Catholic Chaplains). Chaplain Zac was born and raised in Mozambique, Africa. He earned his undergraduate degree in philosophy in Maputo at Saint Augustine Philosophical Seminary. He also has a master's of divinity degree and an MA in theology with concentration in bioethics from Catholic Theological Union in Chicago. Chaplain Zac has provided chaplain services at Deaconess Hospital in Evansville, Indiana, Vitas Hospice Care in Chicago, and Wyoming Medical Center in Casper, Wyoming. Chaplain Zac's diverse cultural understandings provide him a broad perspective when rendering high-quality spiritual assessments and soul care.

FOREWORD

Here we are today, almost two decades into the twenty-first century, and religion and spirituality are still a very important aspect of individual lives around the world. As the world continues to get smaller and smaller, the population continues to rise at almost unsustainable rates. The resources available to meet the needs of this fast-growing population continue to diminish.

However, in the midst of all this change, religion and spirituality continue to thrive and provide a sense of hopefulness for millions of people around the world. People are buoyed by their faith and continue to seek out avenues to practice that faith. While data might suggest that churches, synagogues, mosques, temples, and holy places continue as centers of worship, people are still compelled as religious communities to gather together to practice their sacred beliefs. Still, there are others who do not identify with or feel connected to these ecclesiastical communities and establishments.

As more and more people move away from religious institutional gatherings, they continue to express a desire to have their spiritual needs addressed. Today, there is a strong trend and desire to have that spiritual need addressed in the workplace, where people live 30–40 percent of their lives. In the workplace environment, life goes on and people experience all the joys, excitement, successes, heartaches, struggles, and failures that life brings. In an effort to maintain productivity, corporations and institutions search for ways to address workers' specific religious/spiritual needs so that productivity continues to meet expectations of the organization, board of directors, and shareholders. Many of these corporations, health-care systems, and institutions see the importance of providing for the comfort, care, and spiritual nurture of their workforce. If the workforce is healthy in body, mind, and spirit, then the workforce can wholeheartedly focus on the mission at hand and remain productive. This care that is provided by the workforce employer is done through the profession of chaplaincy.

Chaplaincy is the platform from which ministry is conducted in the workforce today. While chaplaincy as a whole is not faith specific, it nevertheless reaches out to care for the religious and spiritual needs of the workforce built upon specific skill sets that are imperative in the direct hands-on care provided. While chaplaincy is a direct derivative from Christian ministries, today it is practiced from many different religious and spiritual perspectives. Within the academy of chaplaincy, chaplaincy itself is not considered to be faith specific. Chaplains come from many different religious and spiritual traditions to care for the people of their faith group, facilitate for those of other traditions, care for everyone, and advise the workplace leadership and community on religious/spiritual issues, traditions, and holy days as it deals with religious spirituality. Chaplains ministering in these settings need to have finely tuned skill sets in order to fulfill the needs of the people they serve within their own unique workplace settings.

After spending the past forty years in chaplaincy service, I have come to understand the value and importance of finely tuned knowledge, skills, and abilities within the profession of chaplaincy. Having experientially practiced military chaplaincy, law enforcement chaplaincy, and health-care chaplaincy, I can unequivocally support and expound upon the importance of fully developed skill sets for chaplains. Keith Evans has done a masterful job in the publishing of this most important and foundational book, *Essential Chaplain Skills*, as he expounds on the specific skills in the performance of caring for other in times of need and distress.

I am truly humbled that Keith has offered me the distinct privilege of introducing the reader of this work to the field of chaplaincy. Chaplaincy many times is misunderstood and misaligned, as it is coupled with other ministry endeavors. Chaplaincy is an active force in the realm of ministry to a world that is hurting and needing a moment of empathy and an encouraging word of hope.

As Keith Evans lays the initial foundations of chaplaincy, its need, what it is, and who can be a chaplain, he further develops the cornerstone of skills employed in chaplaincy. He very accurately addresses what they are, how they are engaged, what they look like, and what the initial outcomes can be as a result of their employment. This book may very well be one of the first and best of its kind that directly deals with specific chaplain skills and how they are used.

This book is long overdue. Keith has courageously addressed chaplaincy's religious issues without dictating a specific inclusive theological stance. All the while, he remains true to his own Christian faith traditions while emphasizing that chaplaincy is a platform for providing comfort, care, and advice to those who are served by chaplaincy.

From the beginning, we quickly learn and see the emerging role of chaplaincy in this new century. Additionally, we are exposed to the very foundational component of caring and its direct application and impact on the lives of the members of the organization, cooperation, or institution being served. Chaplains, as described in this book, are the foundational instrument of the ministry of care in this twenty-first century and beyond.

To be successful in any endeavor within the workforce, one must master the skills and abilities of the profession one has chosen as a vocation. It is toward that end that I truly and with great pleasure recommend this book as a source of skill development to all professional chaplains, part-time chaplains, volunteer chaplains, seminary/divinity/theological students, and anyone else interested in chaplaincy or the ministry of care. As Keith has stated so poignantly in this book, that many chaplains appreciate the theological point of view espoused by Dietrich Bonhoeffer, "He explained the difference between an *ultimate* versus *penultimate* ministry. Bonhoeffer described *penultimate* as being the 'next to the last word,' eluding that only God has the final or *ultimate* say about anyone's salvation and redemption. This position allows chaplains to simply represent the Sacred, minister to the best of their ability and allow the person an opportunity for deeper faith development" (Evans 2017).

Once again, Keith Evans has communicated masterfully the precise skill sets that chaplains must develop and master. *Essential Chaplain Skills* opens the path to that mastery and the opportunity to touch a life in such a way that changes that life for all of eternity. To God be the glory. Amen.

—Michael W. Langston, DMin
Captain, Chaplain Corps, US Navy (Ret.)
Professor of Chaplaincy
Columbia International University
Columbia, South Carolina

CONTENTS

Preface xiii

Part 1:   The Fundamentals: The Why, What, Who,
             and How of Chaplaincy

Chapter 1:   Why the Need for Chaplains? 1
Chapter 2:   What Is Chaplaincy? 6
Chapter 3:   Who Can Be a Chaplain? 18
Chapter 4:   How is Chaplain Care Administered? 22

Part 2:   Understanding Spirituality
             and World Faith Expressions

Chapter 5:   The Need 39
Chapter 6:   Spirituality of Humanism 50
Chapter 7:   Buddhist Spirituality 65
Chapter 8:   Hindu Spirituality 73
Chapter 9:   Islamic Spirituality 83
Chapter 10: Jewish Spirituality 97
Chapter 11: Christian Spirituality 104

Part 3:   Understanding Spiritual Needs Assessments

Chapter 12: A Paradigm to Understand and Develop
                  Emotional and Spiritual Well-Being 119
Chapter 13: What Is a Spiritual Assessment? 124
Chapter 14: Spiritual Assessment Models 134

Chapter 15: Workplace Spirituality Measurement Tools 147
Chapter 16: Assessing the Spirituality of an Organization
 or Group 157

Part 4: Bringing the Pieces Together

Chapter 17: Bringing the Pieces Together 167
Verbatim 1: Headaches 169
Verbatim 2: Chronic Debilitating Disease 176
Verbatim 3: Do I Stay or Do I Go? 185
Verbatim 4: Emergency Room Death 191
Verbatim 5: A Behavioral Unit Encounter 200
Verbatim 6: Brain Mass 208
Verbatim 7: Hallucinations or Spiritual? 217
Verbatim 8: Fetal Demise 223

Bibliography 239
About the Author 247

PREFACE

Essential Chaplain Skill Sets was originally self-published as three separate e-books entitled *The Chaplain Skillset Series*. This print edition combines the initial three e-book volumes into one text. Additional revisions, edits, and rearrangement of the original material have been made to allow a better flow of reading, understanding, and practical use for teaching environments.

This project emerged from the vast amount of resources that I have gathered throughout my own quest to become the best minister and professional chaplain that I can eventually be. The goal for this text is simply to share well-respected resources and learned lessons, which any chaplain of any faith background in any ministry setting can utilize quickly and effectively. I will speak from my own experiences and from time to time lean heavily upon my own Christian theology to support various chaplain theories, functions, and skill sets. Please understand that it is not my aim to offend any reader from other spirituality or religious doctrines. It is the responsibility of all chaplains to develop their own pastoral identities based upon how their life experiences and their own faith informs them. The various co-contributors share from their faith and belief perspectives.

I am aware that this text is not exhaustive for all the nuances of chaplaincy, but I have strived for it to be as comprehensive as possible in forming an effective foundation. The text has a threefold purpose. It is designed for (1) individuals who are unfamiliar with the unique field of chaplaincy, (2) for laity or clergy who are discerning whether or not to go into chaplain ministry, and (3) for seasoned clergy and chaplains who simply want to revisit the tried and true skill sets, which produce an excellence in chaplaincy. I will always attempt to give credit where credit is due as well as share the many resources that have been helpful in my own chaplain formation.

I hope you enjoy *Essential Chaplain Skill Sets*. If you sift through and dig out just a few pearls of wisdom from each chapter that you can readily use in your own chaplain ministry, then I will consider my efforts to have been worthwhile. May God's peace be upon you as well as upon your specific ministry.

—Chaplain Keith Evans, 2017

PART 1

The Fundamentals: The Why, What, Who, and How of Chaplaincy

CHAPTER 1

Why the Need for Chaplains?

Do you believe there really is a need or place for chaplaincy or chaplains? If there is a need, then is the need only a perceived need for religious people, or is chaplaincy supported by solid anecdotal or qualitative evidence? If there is good information supporting chaplains, what makes chaplains needed? I hope to succinctly answer those questions, plus many more.

The Widening Gap from Organized Faith

Have you truly considered why there is a need for chaplains? A 2016 Gallup Poll (June 14–23) revealed that 89 percent of Americans still believe in a God or universal spirit.[1] This is consistent with a Pew Research study that also states 89 percent of Americans believe in God; however, only about 50 percent of these believers regularly attend any religious services.[2] The most current research compiled by the Barna Group (www.barna.org) reveals that 59 percent of eighteen- to twenty-nine-year-olds with Christian backgrounds have dropped out of attending a church regularly. In 2015, Barna discovered that 25 percent of unchurched adults are skeptical of God's existence,

---

[1] "Most Americans Still Believe in God," *Gallup*, June 29, 2016, accessed May 30, 2017, http://www.gallup.com.
[2] "U.S. Public Becoming Less Religious," November 3, 2015, www.pewforum.org (accessed May 30, 2017).

labeling themselves as either agnostics or atheists. This trend is more predominant in younger adults who are more educated and racially and ethnically diverse. Across gender lines, females are noted as more religiously skeptical than males. Barna states that "the three primary components that lead to disbelief in God's existence [by Skeptics] are 1) rejection of the Bible, 2) a lack of trust in the local church, and 3) the cultural reinforcement of a secular worldview." This information led the Barna Group to develop a "post-Christian metric" that looks at multidimensional factors to describe "the rich and variegated experience of spirituality and faith." Spirituality is indeed diverse and is being defined and expressed in many ways. Anecdotal evidence will also reveal that this trend is occurring throughout all the primary organized faiths: Catholicism, Protestantism, Judaism, etc.

For ministers and chaplains, this data does not come as a surprise but as a validation of the changing expressions of faith and spirituality in America as well as across the globe. With this trend, I have found that the topic of spirituality may be the best place to begin any faith conversation. In fact, it might even prove to be quite difficult to find anyone who would *not* accept the statement that "all humans are spiritual and possess a spirituality, whether they recognize it or not." If you look around and observe your friends, neighbors, and coworkers, you will see individuals who are constantly in search of meaning and purpose in their lives and answers about situations they experience. With so many of the population not active in a local church or organized faith community, there is a great need for effective soul care to be brought to them in their respective places of work by their coworkers and friends—and even by professional workplace chaplains. Chaplains are uniquely qualified to bridge this growing gap in our society, which has pushed back against organized religion yet still strives to find meaning and relevancy in their spiritual selves.

More Evidence for the Need of Chaplains

With more and more emphasis on spirituality at work and other faith movements, there are fewer and fewer individuals sitting in church pews on the Sabbath. This has left a question of who or what becomes a person's spiritual director, pastor, or mentor. It also has left a misunderstanding of what soul care is and what soul care is not.

A definition of spirituality that I espouse, and one that has also been widely received and accepted by most in health-care chaplaincy, was proposed by Dr. Christina Puchalski of the George Washington Institute of Spirituality and Heath. She states that "spirituality is the aspect of humanity that refers to the way individuals seek and express meaning and purpose and the way they experience their connectedness to the moment, to self, to others, to nature, and to the significant or sacred."[3] Others perceive that spirituality stems from one's inner consciousness and is the source behind the outward form of defined religious practices.[4] Religion is more strictly defined as how one's spirituality is practiced within a specific doctrinal or theological context.

In *Care of Souls*, David G. Benner states, "The soul is the meeting point of the psychological and spiritual. Its care must, by necessity, include both spiritual and psychological aspects." In the past century, there have been great strides in understanding the human psyche. But at the same time, the experts have tended to dissect the immaterial self of the individual and divide it up into distinct components (psychological, spiritual, emotional), with each one standing separate and without connection to another. However, there is a growing understanding that this may not be the case. In fact, a dichotomist view of humanity may have more merit in this context

---

[3] Christina M. Puchalski, Robert Vitillo, Sharon K. Hull, and Nancy Reller, "Improving the Spiritual Dimension of Whole Person Care: Reaching National and International Consensus," *Journal of Palliative Medicine* 17, no. 6 (2014): 642.

[4] William A. Guillory, *Spirituality in the Workplace: A Guide for Adapting to the Chaotically Changing Workplace* (Salt Lake City: Innovations International Inc. Publishing, 1997), xi.

of soul care when you assess how individuals cope with crises in their lives. Benner states that we should "understand *soul* as referring to the whole person, including the body, but with particular focus on the inner world of thinking, feeling, and willing. Care of souls can thus be understood as the care of persons in their totality."[5] If the public at large is not engaged in a local church or faith/spirituality community, then who assists people in their journeys? Most often, probably no one.

The work of psychologist Kenneth Pargament has been especially well received within the medical field over the past several decades. Pargament has written extensively on the psychology of an individual's resiliency based upon religion and spirituality as positive coping skills. Pargament's behavioral theories and literature reviews can easily be extrapolated to include individuals under any stress. If you have a scientific tilt to your thinking, then Pargament's *The Psychology of Religion and Coping: Theory, Research, Practice* (1997) will be a great resource for you.

The same can be said of the enormous work of medical physician and researcher Harold Koenig. Koenig's extensive works are *Spirituality and Health Research: Methods, Measurements, Statistics and Resources* (2011) and *Handbook of Spirituality and Health*, second edition (2012). These more academic texts are replete with many categories of scientific data reviews, which support the role and effects of spirituality upon specific physical conditions and mental health issues.

Spirituality has been shown to help a person's overall resiliency after crisis and stress. A 2011 study by Tracy Balboni noted that individuals who have spiritual and religious resources available to them during a time of crisis, such as critical life situations and nearing death itself, actually incur lower overall medical costs.[6] I

---

[5] David B. Benner, *Care of Souls: Revisioning Christian Nurture and Counsel* (Grand Rapids: Baker Books, 1998), 22.

[6] Tracy Balboni, et al, "Support of Cancer Patient's Spiritual Needs and Associations with Medical Care Costs at the End of Life," *Cancer* 117 (2011): 5383–91. http://www.ncbi.nlm.nih.gov/pmc/articles/PMC3177963.

infer from this study that the individuals became less anxious and more emotionally and psychologically relaxed when they felt more supported and less vulnerable. As this occurred, there was less need for anxiety or pain medications, which led to the patients' better comfort and rest and even increased healing rates because their immune systems improved. When this occurs, the patient will often have a shorter length of stay and better satisfaction with his or her overall care!

A survey of the American Hospital Association's database noted "significantly lower rates of hospital deaths ($\beta=0.4$, $p<.05$) and higher rates of hospice enrollment ($\beta =.06$, $p<.001$) for patients cared for in hospitals that provided chaplaincy services than in hospitals that did not."[7] The study noted that the results "may be attributable to chaplain's assistance to patients and families in making decisions about care at the end-of-life, perhaps by aligning their values and wishes with actual treatment plans."[8]

Spirituality is vastly important to the resiliency and maintenance of emotional well-being and wholeness for individuals, while organized religion is being more and more opposed. If this is true, then what or who is the best possible facilitator to assist those in need? From my perspective, the chaplain is the most reasonable bridge builder and available public clergy when much of the population does not belong to or attend a church on a regular basis. For the multitude of people with spiritual needs who are also on quests for their own deeper meaning and purpose in life, the well-equipped and skilled chaplain may well prove to be their best spiritual mentor.

---

[7] Kevin J. Flannelly, et al, "A National Study of Chaplaincy Services and End of Life Outcomes," *BMC Palliative Care* 11, no. 10 (2012): 1, accessed September 1, 2013, http://biomedcentral.com/1472-684x/11/10.

[8] Ibid., 6.

CHAPTER 2

What Is Chaplaincy?

Chaplain—Liaison and Minister of Presence

Let's now look into discovering a better understanding of what chaplaincy is, and maybe through understanding what chaplaincy is, you may even understand what chaplaincy is not. Chaplaincy is public ministry that serves others who are in spiritual and emotional need. While each chaplain will possess his or her own theology and be endorsed by a specific faith tradition, chaplaincy ministry is not denominational or faith-specific.

Chaplaincy is not about converting others to the chaplain's faith; it's about the chaplain's ability to "emotionally and spiritually connect to," "be with," and "serve" the other as appropriate and permitted. This often requires relationship building, and it is permission based. For example, I am a hospital chaplain. I possess the authority to walk into any room and introduce myself and speak to employees, patients, family members, and physicians. But it will be the relationship, rapport, and trust with others, which develop beyond my initial "authority," that give me the continued permission to stay there and offer the ministry of soul care.

I asked a close chaplain friend, who is of African ethnicity and trained in hospital and hospice chaplaincy, how he would answer the question, "What is chaplaincy?" Chaplain Zacarias Buhuro gave a great, succinct description:

> A chaplain is someone in journey with the patients and families. A chaplain is not a fixer or an answer giver. A chaplain provides a unique presence to patients and families, a presence that allows them to show their deep vulnerability of being human while facing a diagnosis that may lead to terminal illness. A chaplain should be able to approach patients and families simultaneously with an agenda and without any agenda—an agenda to engage patients and families in distress situations or facing terminal illness and after they have been told "you have six months or less to live."

During our conversations, Zac would often remind me and others, that even though the chaplain is a religious/spiritual representative, he or she should approach without any agenda and not assume and "bring" a God, religious, and spirituality agenda to patients. God and hope are already there before the chaplain encounters patients and families.

A chaplain is a pastoral and spiritual counselor, advocate, and guide. A chaplain should start from where the patient and family's "here and now" and use their religious beliefs, after an assessment, to articulate hope, despair, and effective coping options. A chaplain should not judge a patient or a family's religious beliefs, nonbeliefs, sexual orientation, race, and origin but facilitate the expression of feelings and provide active, empathetic listening to patients and families. A chaplain should provide an assuring presence to families that may be feeling guilty that they did not do enough for their loved ones or allow patients to die while assuring them that their loved ones will be "okay" and that it is all right to die.

A chaplain has to be comfortable to talk about death and dying. Doing so will assist the families and patients who may be reluctant to even approach or discuss the proverbial elephant in the room: death. A chaplain is a liaison with local churches, synagogues, and mosques. Ultimately, a chaplain should be open-minded, flexible, cross-culturally sensitive, and understanding. I believe Chaplain Zac has an excellent grasp on what chaplaincy is to him and should be to others.

Chaplain Keith Evans

Theology for Soul Care and Chaplaincy

In my own journey into chaplaincy, I looked for a philosophy or theoretical premise, which might serve as a road map toward a theoretical basis and application of soul care and chaplaincy. I am aware that my perspective and theological basis may not align perfectly with all readers. I respect that. I trust that you do as well, but I do hope that these primary theological principles that I have embraced will also be considered and recognized as having merit with any chaplain's faith or spirituality tradition.

A Theological Premise for Chaplaincy

One of the great stories in scripture is the parable of the Good Samaritan as told by Jesus (Luke 10:25–37). When I was in my early twenties, my pastor was Dr. Joel Gregory. Dr. Gregory's account of this story still stirs my soul today, and fortunately for myself and many others, the sermon can still be digitally downloaded and is outlined in his text *Gregory's Sermon Synopses.* In full disclosure, much of my thinking on this premise as a foundation for chaplaincy ministry is afforded to Dr. Gregory's study. For me, the role of chaplains, who are ministers in the public sector, mirror many of the attitude and intentional actions of the Good Samaritan. If you are not that familiar with the story, let me present it to you in the New King James Version translation:

> And behold, a certain lawyer stood up and tested Him, saying, "Teacher, what shall I do to inherit eternal life?" He said to him, "What is written in the law? What is your reading of it?" So he answered and said, "You shall love the LORD your God with all your heart, with all your soul, with all your strength, and with all your mind,' and 'your neighbor as yourself." And He said to him, "You have answered rightly; do this and you will live." But he, wanting to justify himself, said to Jesus, "And who is my neighbor?" Then Jesus answered and said: "A certain man went down

from Jerusalem to Jericho, and fell among thieves, who stripped him of his clothing, wounded him, and departed, leaving him half dead. Now by chance a certain priest came down that road. And when he saw him, he passed by on the other side. Likewise a Levite, when he arrived at the place, came and looked, and passed by on the other side. But a certain Samaritan, as he journeyed, came where he was. And when he saw him, he had compassion. So he went to him and bandaged his wounds, pouring on oil and wine; and he set him on his own animal, brought him to an inn, and took care of him. On the next day, when he departed, he took out two denarii, gave them to the innkeeper, and said to him, 'Take care of him; and whatever more you spend, when I come again, I will repay you.' So which of these three do you think was neighbor to him who fell among the thieves?" And he said, "He who showed mercy on him." Then Jesus said to him, "Go and do likewise." (Luke 10:25-37 NKJV)

As you analyze the characters of the story, you will first notice two people. The one referred to as a Jewish teacher is Jesus, and the other is a Jewish lawyer. The lawyer, who is very well versed in the ancient Jewish laws of the Torah and who has been thinking upon his own mortality, asks the Teacher what he must *do* to *inherit* eternal life. The wise Teacher responds to the posed question with a counter question and inquired of the astute lawyer as to what the lawyer already knows the law to say. For the lawyer, he did not need to look further than between his own eyes. Per the Jewish tradition, strict Jewish men wore phylacteries, which were small leather boxes that held prominent passages from the Torah and were often worn like a headband. This man knew the Jewish law by memory.

The lawyer responded, quoting the Jewish Shema from the sixth chapter of Deuteronomy: "You shall love the Lord your God with all your heart, with all your soul, with all your strength, and with all your mind" (Deuteronomy 6:4-5 NKJV) and to love and treat "your neighbor as yourself" as affirmed in Leviticus 19:18. The

Teacher heard his response and essentially gave him a thumbs-up and encouraged him to just go and do this. Yet the lawyer seemed to need more clarification to understand. He wanted to know who *is* his neighbor and *to whom* was he to show such compassion, care, and love. Who is the one near me that I am to be neighborly toward? If that was difficult to know to this man in ancient times, think about the complexities of that question in our contemporary and global community? I suspect the lawyer's next thought was how he should treat them.

As I read this, I thought, *Really?* Do you know people like this who just seem to not get it? It is as though the lawyer needed justification and direction to what his actions should be in order to inherit eternal life. This is when the wise Teacher spins the direction of the quest of the lawyer from a mechanistic action for salvation and transforms it to a very personal and pinpoint attitude and intention, which the lawyer should possess. The Teacher shares a story that held all the truths and heart's attitude the lawyer (and you and me) needs to understand.

Jesus may have actually been on this road from Jerusalem to Jericho when he shared the story. If so, it would have even made the story even more dramatic as the listeners could have easily imagined themselves as one of the story's characters. This story was practical and well understood by the listeners of that day. The tale takes place along a hard, desolate road. Geographically, the road descended more than three thousand feet over the approximately twenty miles between the City on the Hill and Jericho.

One day, a traveler was heading down this road. Robbers and thugs often hung out in this wasteland to take advantage of unprotected passersby. On this unfortunate day, the traveler was indeed stopped by a roaming gang of thugs. He was robbed, beaten, and left to die in a ditch by the road.

A Jewish priest eventually passed by. One would think that a religious man would have compassion. The religious leader saw the unconscious man, and without breaking stride or even checking on the man, kept walking by. Was it the religious restrictions of the priest that may have kept him from touching a potential corpse? Did he feel that he just did not have time to attend to this obvious need? We are not told. But we do know that the priest just kept walking by.

A Levite then approached and saw the wounded man. You would think the church deacon would help, right? Not in this situation. Maybe he was busy or late for an appointment that was more important. We do not know. Maybe the deacon cynically thought, *Wow, poor guy. He should have known better. He should have protected himself better. I am sure he brought this on himself. Maybe he is a robber himself?* Or maybe he thought in our modern-day thinking and decided to form a research study to see what is wrong with the road. *Can a new local agency be formed to collect funds to assist with these difficult rural-community needs?* We are not sure what crossed through this churchgoer's mind—we only know that he kept walking just as the religious leader did.

The listening lawyer and group around the Teacher may have expected the third person of this story to be a righteous, pious fellow countryman, which would have followed the good storytelling principles of that day, but Jesus surprised the listening group by stating the third person who stopped was a scandalous character to the locals. Most people of that time would have soon have suffered and died in the ditch rather than receive help from a detestable Samaritan man. The Samaritans were the ethnically mixed offspring of Jewish and Assyrian intermarriages. Jews of that era avoided Samaritans like they were the plague.

Jesus said the Samaritan felt compassion for the man in the ditch. The Samaritan did not switch sides of the road as the priest or Levite did. He physically went over and down into the ditch in order to assist the man who was in desperate need. The Samaritan did this without preconceived assumptions or judgment of the man or his character. He simply attended to him out of respect for him as a fellow human in need. At the close of the story, the Teacher tells the lawyer to *go* and *become* a neighbor to everyone just as the Good Samaritan did.

How does this relate and support a chaplain's role and ministry? Principles from the Good Samaritan parable that relate to chaplaincy are abundant! Who is your neighbor? Is your neighbor the person living next door or the individual you work with? Yes. Can your neighbor be someone other than your own race or ethnicity? They should be. Do your neighbors include the homeless lady sleeping on the park bench (by her choice or otherwise), the addict, the abuser, or even the rich couple down the street? Based upon the Samaritan story, all these people mentioned should be considered your neighbor.

So what innately makes anyone your neighbor? One might say they are neighbors simply because they are humans with unalienable rights as such. For me, they are my neighbors because they all were uniquely created by an almighty and powerful God, which gives them value, worth, and unalienable rights from above. In biblical language, this is the *imago dei* (Genesis 1:26–27). I may not agree with their decisions in life, but I can respect them and care for their core needs because they were uniquely created and given life by God. This is how chaplains respond toward individuals of diverse cultures, ethnicity, lifestyles, and needs. It all begins with an inner attitude of understanding who your neighbor is and what it means to be neighborly.

Another principle of this story, which is directly applicable for chaplains, is that the Good Samaritan had compassion upon a down-and-out person who was in desperate need of assistance. Others had passed the man due to their daily schedules or fears. The Good Samaritan stopped and used his own resources to get him to a place that could care for him better, and he even sacrificed his own monetary resources to pay for extra care beyond that which he could give. In essence, chaplains do this on a daily basis within their own context and the people they serve. It may be more time and emotional and spiritual support, but chaplains also serve as liaisons in obtaining resources those in need require, just as the Good Samaritan did. To avoid getting too preachy, I will stop here and allow you to further your study on the parable of the Good Samaritan on your own. I highly suggest that every reader do this intellectual and spiritually enlightening effort.

Establishing a Theoretical Basis for Chaplaincy

Pastor Rick Warren poses a strategic question in *The Purpose Driven Church*. Warren challenges every ministry (whether it is congregational, parachurch religious, or an independent chaplain ministry) to ask two important questions: "Why *do* we exist?" and "Why *should* we exist?" Until the ministry and minister fully understands this, there may not be any foundation, motivation, or direction for the ministry. Until the ministry or minister fully understands what and who they are, as well as what their impact may be to a hurting world, then how can the minister or ministry group ever really implement an effective action plan to achieve their goals? This is very true for all chaplains and organizations that use chaplains.

I agree with the ancient scriptures that the objective core function of any ministry is to serve others while glorifying God in all endeavors (Romans 15:6; 1 Corinthians 10:31; Ephesians 1:14). As a Christian chaplain, the nature, tasks, and authority that guide me as a chaplain stem from the Holy Scriptures. If you are a chaplain of another faith group, I suspect you too will hold fast to your theology and will want to discover the doctrines of your faith, which support your role as a minister. These deep truths produce your own spiritual formation, which develops your pastoral identity.

Chaplaincy ministry service of any setting may be defined as spiritual assessment and intervention that is not agenda driven or denominationally specific. The spiritual care of chaplaincy is meeting and being with people in crisis and connecting with them where they are emotionally and spiritually. In the parish setting, the practice and art of pastoral care can be very intentional and more focused where faith values are generally already understood and shared between clergy and parishioner. In the ecumenical and/or interfaith setting of public ministry, spiritual care takes on a different role and approach.

One pastoral care theory or theology that many chaplains appreciate was espoused by Dietrich Bonhoeffer. He explained the difference between *ultimate* and *penultimate* ministry.[9] Bonhoeffer described *penultimate* as being the "next to the last word" since only God has the final or *ultimate* say about anyone's salvation and redemption. This position allows chaplains to simply represent the sacred, minister to the best of their ability, and allow the person an opportunity for deeper faith development.

James Fowler views a person's faith as being a verb, and it is equated with making sense out of life, but it is not always associated with any one religion or denomination label (Fowler, 1981). Fowler states that people are in search for something that loves us, something to value that gives us value, something to honor and respect that has power to sustain our being—all that makes life worth living. Scriptures reveal that God knows and understands the hearts of all men (1 Kings 8:39; Psalm 20:4; 37:4; 145:19; Jeremiah 17:9–10). God knows the heart of believers.

As ministers come to understand this penultimate posture of ministry, meaningful spiritual encounters can occur between two persons who may even exhibit diametrically opposed theologies. This theological position is an effective way to render spiritual care. For chaplaincy, this position allows the chaplain to simply be real and present—and allow God to work as He chooses.

Chaplains might even consider their approach to that of being a foreign missionary. Every person has a story and is a story in the making. For chaplains rendering pastoral care outside of formal religious confines, it is indeed a missionary mentality of being Christ to a hurting world. Chaplains listen to life stories, hurts, and victories. Chaplains help direct troubled souls to discover meaning and purpose of their lives.

Every person possesses some form of religious beliefs and practices. These beliefs and practices can be tightly interwoven with cultural contexts. It is in these situations that chaplains constitute a powerful

---

[9] Dietrich Bonhoeffer, *Ethics* (New York: Macmillan Publishing Company, 1955), 120–132.

reminder of the healing, sustaining, guiding, and reconciling power of one's faith.[10]

Good soul care presents itself to the whole person. In times of loss and crisis, the patient's material and immaterial selves (psycho, emotional, spiritual) are all intertwined. The effective chaplain needs to have at least a general-to-moderate understanding of the human condition, which can assist them in providing good grief work, bereavement, and acute crisis management from a biblical standpoint. Being able to adequately assess the individual's emotional and cognitive mental state is paramount in conducting a proper spiritual assessment and discovering how faith lends to or hinders their life situations.

After the chaplain assesses the person's basic mental status, cognition, and general ability to properly communicate, are they even willing to converse about spiritual matters? This permission can only be given by the other person. Without it, a spiritual care encounter will be limited—or the chaplain will have to look for other ways to connect and build a trusting rapport with the individual.

The functions of the universal church (as well as for ministers and chaplains) are timeless, unchanging, nonnegotiable, and purposeful. They can also be viewed as biblically mandated.[11] The core functions are worship, fellowship, teaching, evangelism, and service. For chaplains, their function is the same as the church, but they function outside of the church walls. For chaplains, they represent the sacred and divine as they function a "ministry of presence" and "service" to others in need.

The mode or form of the core functions may widely vary in different cultures, geographical locations, and societies. Forms are negotiable, changeable, and cultural. Various appropriate methodologies should be considered when ministry contexts are outside of the norm. Good

---

[10] Larry VandeCreek and Laurel Burton, *Professional Chaplaincy: Its Role and Importance in Healthcare* (Schaumburg, IL: Association of Professional Chaplains, 2001), 8.

[11] Aubrey Malphurs, *A New Kind of Church: Understanding Models of Ministry for the 21st Century* (Grand Rapids, MI: Baker Books, 2007), 76–79.

spiritual soul care will discover and address what is meaningful to the identified individual. Jesus is commonly referred to as being the itinerant minister. He genuinely reacted to people's expressed needs.

The chaplain needs to discover if the other person has meaningful religious rituals and faith traditions (sacramental or symbolic), which the chaplain can assist. In a hospital setting, this may include specific death or other ethnic rituals associated with illness, death, and loss. As the chaplain recognizes that religious and ethnic rituals can be very comforting during a time of crisis and emotional disorganization, then that awareness will lead their ministry toward increased effectiveness. Professional chaplains reach across faith-group boundaries and do not proselytize. Acting on behalf of the chaplain's institution, "they also seek to protect patients from being confronted by other, unwelcome, forms of spiritual intrusion."[12] This principle should be true in any workplace chaplain setting, whether it be law enforcement, emergency first responders, industrial, or corporate.

Just as medical treatments require a patient's consent to be administered, pastoral care should be handled with the same attitude. The mindful and confident chaplain can be a great asset to any organization, but the chaplain must be mindful to not over-function or overstep one's jurisdiction within the organization. Being sensitive and respectful to delicate emotional and spiritual conditions of people is highly important. If not, then the chaplain's use of pastoral authority could be questioned.

Another guiding principle in the philosophy of soul care and chaplaincy is to do all things in love and compassion, as displayed in the parable of the Good Samaritan. Loving and treating another human being for simply being another human being is what Jesus modeled in the Scriptures (Matthew 22:39). Demonstrating the Golden Rule within the administration of good pastoral care is meeting them where they are, despite any personal, political, sociological,

---

[12] VandeCreek and Burton, 8.

theological, or religious differences. The more self-differentiated the chaplain is, the better the administered soul care will be.

Providing an effective ministry in a diverse population is to be aware of psychological alignment. This is a technique often used in pastoral crisis intervention. Aligning oneself (agreeing or expressing that at least you understand their situation or perspective) with the other individual's ideals or emotional situation allows the individual to remain empowered and in control and not feel defensive or marginalized. The concept of alignment should not be confused with endorsement or considered "reverse psychology." Alignment is merely a technique to avoid counterproductive confrontation, argument, or alienation, and subsequent communication breakdown. When done correctly, it opens a door to constructive dialogue and can generate more adaptive coping options.[13]

For me, the revelation of Jesus Christ through Word and action is at the heart of mission and all chaplaincy soul care. I often ask myself, "Can this level of soul care be rendered by non-Christian chaplains?" Honestly, I would have to say, "Yes." My theology informs me that the power of God is immense, and this divine power can flow through any person for God's grand purpose and glory. Good chaplains will discover the needed bridges of their ministry setting. This will allow the nonreligious as well as seasoned church attendees to cross over and meet one another in spiritual moments. More of these types of "best practices" and bridges will be discussed in a following chapter.

At the core of soul care is the truth that all people have worth and dignity. Each individual's faith expression is an essential dimension to his or her own wholeness. If there is a need as well as a desire for spiritual and soul care to be available to all individuals despite their traditional faith origin, then the chaplain has a great responsibility ahead of them.

---

[13] George S. Everly, *Pastoral Crisis Intervention: Course Workbook* (Ellicott City, MD: Chevron Press), 2002.

CHAPTER 3

Who Can Be a Chaplain?

To truly define who can be a chaplain, the best method may be to look at the most recognized methods and where chaplains are used the most. If I asked ten people "Where do chaplains exist or work?" I would suspect that at least eight or nine of the ten would immediately connect chaplains with the military or with hospitals. And that would be correct since chaplains have been with those institutions the longest. But there are many more places and organizations that are now using chaplains on a regular basis.

If you are considering entering into chaplaincy, then I loudly applaud you. Many volunteer chaplains may not possess specific religious education and credentials. However, their intuition and guidance from God often places them well above other seasoned and credentialed chaplains. If you are ordained, ecclesiastically endorsed, have completed 1,600-plus hours of clinical pastoral education (CPE), and meet the high standards of pastoral care competencies to become a board-certified professional chaplain, then please assume that I am now saluting you and giving you a standing ovation!

Military and health-care chaplains have essentially set the standards for what professional chaplaincy has become and how it presents itself. These fields are the gold standard to which all other chaplaincy areas are and will continue to be compared. I do not view this as a bad thing. If you are thinking about entering into full-time

Essential Chaplain Skill Sets

chaplaincy, this short section will give you much to consider and will hopefully smooth the path of discernment you are now journeying.

A quick Internet search on job descriptions and preferred qualifications for a hospital or health-care chaplain reveals the growing preference by organizations to seek chaplain candidates who possess religious education, ordination, and/or ecclesiastical endorsement by their religious denomination and ministry experience. Many job descriptions will also list the preference for applicants to have completed at least one unit of a specialized internship program of CPE. Pragmatically, chaplain candidates with four or more CPE units and religious degrees are normally hired at larger private, nonprofit, and state-run health-care organizations.

Several well-respected national chaplain organizations evaluate and board certify chaplains in professional chaplaincy. All of these organizations have established ethical and professional standards and share many of the same competencies (more than thirty) for chaplains to possess in order to become board certified. These organizations are a wonderful resource: the Association of Professional Chaplains (APC), the Canadian Association of Spiritual Care (CASC), the National Association of Catholic Chaplains (NACC), Neshama: the National Association of Jewish Chaplains (NAJC), the National Association of Veteran's Affairs Chaplains (NAVAC), the National Conference of Veteran's Affairs Catholic Chaplains (NCVACC), the Healthcare Chaplains Ministry Association (HCMA), and the Spiritual Care Association (SCA). The professional spiritual care competencies that are adopted and supported by a majority of these organizations are categorized into four general categories; (1) the integration of theory and practice competencies, (2) professional identify and conduct competencies, (3) professional practice skills competencies, and (4) organizational leadership competencies.[14]

Often the seasoned minister does well with the competencies

---

[14] "Common Qualifications and Competencies for Professional Chaplains," Association of Professional Chaplains www.professionalchaplains.org (accessed on May 9, 2017).

of theory and professional pastoral identity but may need to learn the role of effective pastoral soul care and unique professional competencies required for on "outside-of-the-church walls" public chaplain ministry. Per these professional chaplain competencies, the professional chaplain candidate will be able to articulate a theology of spiritual care that is integrated into their theory of pastoral practice. The candidate will also possess an understanding and ability to incorporate a working knowledge of psychological and sociological disciplines, diverse religious beliefs and practices in the provision of pastoral care, and the ability to understand and utilize the spiritual and emotional dimensions of human development into the practice of pastoral care. Can the chaplain function pastorally in a manner that respects the physical, emotional, and spiritual boundaries of others and articulate ways in which one's feelings, attitudes, values, and assumptions affect one's pastoral care? Most chaplains have the gift for advocacy and compassion. Chaplains also need to be proficient communicating well—orally and in writing—while respecting and functioning in diverse situations of culture, gender, sexual orientation, and spiritual/religious practices.

From the professional competency category, the chaplain needs to possess professionalism and leadership skills in integrating "pastoral and spiritual care into the life and service of the institution in which it resides," skills to "establish and maintain professional and interdisciplinary relationship," and "support, promote and encourage ethical decision making and care." All these professional competencies, and more, can be found on the websites of the listed national certifying organizations. If you are in a discernment process of considering chaplaincy, I would highly encourage you to truly self-reflect upon your strengths and weaknesses and identify what learning areas you may need to improve upon.

If you are not being led to enter into a process toward professional chaplain certification, any amount of self-learning will assist you well. There are many great texts on pastoral care or soul care. Some of the great authors who have shaped this field include Steward Hiltner, Wayne Oates, Edward H. Thorton, and Howard Clinebell. Other leading experts who have authored texts useful to many areas of pastoral soul care and chaplaincy who may prove helpful to explore include Howard W. Stone, Ken Doka, Jung Young Lee, Frederick W. Schmidt, Sonya Ely Wheeler, James Fowler, Brene' Brown, Edwin H. Friedman, Clara Hill, and David Augsburger. Of course, many others exist as well.

CHAPTER 4

How is Chaplain Care Administered?

Many chaplains possess an innate internal guidance and giftedness for chaplaincy ministry. That is why they are so good in this ministry. But despite a natural or ordained bent to do the ministry well, it is always advisable to review the basic fundamentals. In this practical chapter, I will touch upon a dozen of the most needed skill sets I have observed to become proficient.

The No-Agenda Approach

1. Knowing Oneself

A key element to not having an agenda other than being with people and seeing what happens is to truly know yourself and your own faith beliefs. A psychologist might label this as the chaplain being "self-differentiated." This self-differentiation is the ability to be in the presence of intense emotion and opposition without being personally offended. It is knowing oneself. It is recognizing and labeling your own emotions as they might swell up but not allowing your own emotions or thoughts to thwart your ministry to the other person.

Chaplains should never minister with an intent to debate or evangelize, but chaplains should answer direct questions about faith and theology when asked. You may not agree with me on this, and that is fine. I fully understand the reasoning. However, if you are not a skilled, high-level diplomat, just answer the other person's question. To do so will show respect to them. I have witnessed chaplains skirting around answering more personal questions, but so often, the conversation just becomes really awkward. I would rather simply answer the question, keeping it short and to the point, and then diplomatically redirect the conversation back toward the other person's needs. From my perspective and experience, answering a direct question will not thwart the soul care opportunity and should actually build rapport and trust if it is handled honestly, calmly, and respectfully.

Maintaining the no-agenda approach allows chaplains to serve as a liaison for resources the other individual may need to better cope and spiritually deal with in his or her current situation. The chaplain's role is not to give long-term psychotherapy but to be available to give sage advice about life and faith when called upon.

2. Attentive Listening Skills

"He who answers a matter before he hears it, It is folly and shame to him" (Proverbs 18:13 NKJV). Chaplains must listen and be patient while doing so! It has been said that listening is the greatest compliment you can give another person. This is where good communication begins. A key phrase in starting a conversation may be a derivative of an open-ended question: "Tell me your story. What is going on?" Listening for concerns is paramount to offering good soul care. Also, listen with your eyes and observe body language, emotions, and where their energy and thoughts are directed in the conversation. These are all jumping-off points for more in-depth and potentially deeper emotional and spiritual conversations. Good attentive listening will help avoid an agenda-driven, mechanistic approach, which may well be viewed as routine, cold, and uncaring by the other individual.

3. Restating, Reinterpreting, and Using Open-Ended Questions

These are much-needed skill sets for chaplains. The skill of restating what you have heard is vital to allow the other person to know that you are indeed listening and hearing what they are trying to convey to you. Restating or paraphrasing what you heard in a slightly different way can be very useful. This method can also offer more ways for the other people to express themselves. Also, a break in the conversation—as you rephrase and restate—may allow them time to think and process what they are dealing with emotionally or even consider making more clarifying statements to clear up any misunderstandings.

Be cautious to not remain too superficial and parrot back exactly what they just shared with you. Examples of a restatement might include: "I hear that you're saying that your parents are divorcing" or "To summarize, you seem clearer about what you are deciding to do about your father's medical options."

Reinterpreting the information back to the individual often helps shed a new perspective upon the situation that may not have already been considered. It also helps clarify what the chaplain has heard and lets the other person know he or she is being heard and understood.

Avoid asking simple questions that may only elicit a yes or no response. Using this type of simple question can easily shut conversations down, and the chaplain will lose the ability to develop trust and rapport with the individual, which ultimately loses the opportunity for ministry and influence. A better way is using open-ended questions. Open-ended questions are questions that prompt more explanation and dialogue. In essence, use a short question that provokes a long answer. My popular "What happened?" is an excellent open-ended question to start a conversation with someone you do not know. This method easily allows non-touchy-feely people to express their full range of emotions within the story narrative and not feel threatened by a stranger trying to "counsel" them or "get into their head." Just let them share and stay engaged with them in the story.

Chaplaincy is often about psychological triage or psychological first aid (PFA). These are simple methods to invite others who are in stress or crisis and help emotionally (and spiritually) process what they are experiencing. I will discuss this topic of psychological first aid in much greater detail in a future volume. It would be very prudent for any chaplain to study techniques and open-ended questions. I would highly recommend all readers to access a copy of Clara E. Hill's *Helping Skills: Facilitating, Exploration, Insight, and Action*. Hill's work is excellent. The most excellent chaplain will learn to possess these wonderful skill sets!

4. Be Spiritually Intentional in Conversations

Below are some other general dos and don'ts of chaplain conversations I have picked up throughout the years. Social conversations focus on the superficial, and chaplain soul care conversations will intentionally focus and be directed toward the here and now as well as upon the other person and not the chaplain.

Four examples:

1. Social conversations tend to concentrate on external subjects such as the weather and local and world events, while soul care conversation concentrates upon the person in front of you.
2. Social conversation concentrates on comfort through avoiding speaking about the obvious crisis or situation, while soul care conversations concentrate on seeking comfort by facing fears and present circumstances.
3. Social conversation concentrates upon the "what should be" while the soul care conversation focuses upon the "what is."
4. Social conversations often are only helpful by providing distraction through entertainment, but soul care conversations seek helpfulness through intimate sharing.

5. Meet Their Needs, Not Yours

Through a respectful and intentional conversation, you will discover the needs of the other person. Once a need is discovered, ask for permission to help. The expressed need may not be anything spiritual or religious in nature. That is okay. Your presence and attentive listening provide needed ministry and service. If they need a cup of water, be Christ to them and arrange for a cup of water! There will be times when they still may not want your assistance. If so, respect their wishes. Chaplaincy is truly about the autonomy and respect of the other person. Do not break that trust.

On a side note, it should go without saying that chaplaincy ministry is not for the evangelist! Unless the evangelistic nature is tamed, the "chaplain" will not be doing chaplaincy but will be following their own agenda, which breaks rule number one of maintaining a no-agenda approach. Plus, in our current postmodern age, most adults prefer to know how their spirituality or God is relevant in their lives than you telling them what they should be doing and thinking. If you have a secret agenda to share your story to every person you meet, you will not be doing chaplaincy. Always strive to meet their immediate needs and not your own.

6. Use Neutral Communication Language

For chaplains, it is normally advisable to talk to others using neutral religious theological language. If you grew up in a church and have become very strong in your faith tradition, you might not realize how much religious language you use on a daily basis. First impressions are everything in the chaplain world. If you speak like you are a robotic theological dictionary and seminary professor, most people will tune you out in a nanosecond! As soon as they do, you have lost any chance for the influence and assistance you may have had for them.

This is why I highly recommend that you consider removing all religious lingo and theological phrases from your vocabulary when you are initially engaging and developing a rapport and trust with someone. It is never useful to talk when others do not understand you! The chaplain conversation should be about them and not you validating your presence as clergy or your knowledge of theology. Why? Religious and theological language and terms is a hotbed of potential misunderstandings! It is always best to use nonreligious language.

Since this text is not a chaplain encounter with someone, if you will allow me, I would like to spend more time discussing this topic from a deeper philosophical and theological perspective. This concept has been discussed and named by George Lindbeck as a cultural-linguistic approach. Others have written on this as well. Lindbeck's theology behind his concept may not sit well with all faith groups, but I see the superficial, pragmatic utility of his concept as a great principle for a chaplain's interfaith conversations.

Allow me to expound upon the practical usage of Lindbeck's concept. Lindbeck's life work held a major interest in ecumenical dialogue, especially regarding Lutheran-Roman Catholic dialogue. With respect to this special interest, Lindbeck was appointed to serve as a representative of the Lutheran World Federation for all four sessions of Vatican II from 1962 until 1965. One of the texts he wrote on ecumenical dialogue is *The Nature of Doctrine: Religion and Theology in a Postliberal Age*. Lindbeck's thesis argues that theories of religion and doctrines are derived from "philosophical and social-scientific approaches" and not specifically from Christian, biblical, or ecumenical posits. It is from this perspective that Lindbeck argues a cultural-linguistic approach is a better method for ecumenical and even nonreligious discussions altogether. Embracing this concept can be of great importance for professional chaplains. Developing the skill set may actually be a priceless competency.

Lindbeck bases his argument upon a rule theory of doctrine. His logic states that prior cultural experience shapes the entirety of a person's life and thoughts. If this is so, then experience forms religious doctrinal statements, which then act as rules determining the language any given community will accept as proper regarding theological matters. In essence, Lindbeck states that the culture of experiences defines the meaning behind words and language. Of course, this is exactly how postmodernism and relativism functions.

Lindbeck sees a cultural problem of religious pluralism because there is no preset definition or meaning to religious language. Due to the various meanings placed upon religious terms, he states,

> This lack of a common foundation is a weakness, but is also a strength. It means, that on one hand, that the partners in dialogue do not start with the conviction that they really basically agree, but it also means that they are not forced into the dilemma of thinking of themselves as representing a superior (or an inferior) articulation of a common experience of which other religions are inferior (or superior) expressions.[15]

In reviewing Lindbeck's idea, scholar Tasi Perkins cautions,

> It is humanistically useful, but it must be done carefully and non-teleologically in order to avoid the transgressions that it will nevertheless inevitably commit. Lindbeck exhorted, with a caveat, "The missionary task of Christians may at times be to encourage Marxists to become better Marxists, Jews and Muslims to become better Jews and Muslims, and Buddhists to become better Buddhists (although admittedly their notion of what a 'better Marxist,' etc., is will be influenced by Christian norms)."[16]

Richard Pruitt agrees with Lindbeck that the secular world is not interested in theological or doctrinal applications but is more interested in the underlying motivation of religious behavior.

---

[15] George A. Lindbeck, *The Nature of Doctrine: Religion and Theology in a Postliberal Age* (Philadelphia: Westminster, 1984), 55.
[16] Tasi Perkins, "Beyond Jacques Derrida and George Lindbeck: Toward a Particularity-Based Approach to Interreligious Communication," *Journal of Ecumenical Studies*, (June 2013) 48:3, pages unknown. http://www.thefreelibrary.com (accessed March 21, 2014).

> Lindbeck, however, sees within the language of the secular arena's observation and fascination with religion the most promising method of bridging the ever-widening gap between the (fundamentalist and evangelical) propositionalists and the (liberal) experiential-expressivists.[17]

For me, neutralizing theological language to a more common verbiage without removing the deeper meaning is very helpful when approaching individuals unfamiliar to theology. Using this method for pre-evangelism and for stimulating more biblical-based and spiritual conversations should be highly effective. This skill set of using neutral religious and theological language during public ministry should be considered by all chaplains.

7. Assist in Emotional Processing

Chaplains who gain the knowledge of administering psychological first aid can be used in very powerful ways. As previously mentioned, psychological first aid or psychological triage is a process for assisting a person who is in intense emotional and spiritual distress. People in the midst of intense shock and crisis cannot think straight. We have all experienced this in one form or another. Our emotions totally overwhelm our ability to cognitively think clearly. The process helps them to regain their mental composure and cognitive-thinking abilities.

There are many two-day training courses on this form of assistance (i.e., mental health first aid, psychological first aid, critical incident stress management techniques for individuals, pastoral crisis intervention). A chaplain who develops this level of training and skill sets will have many tools available to assist people in almost any situation. This area of helping manage critical stress situations will be discussed in another volume in much greater detail.

---

[17] Perkins, 3.

8. Learn Local Religious and Community Resources that You Cannot Offer

The Good Samaritan was not able to offer all the resources to the wounded man in need. But the Good Samaritan did know who could, and he made the appropriate arrangements and contacts. Chaplains should do the same. This should go without saying that, if you are not a Catholic priest, do not offer a Catholic sacrament. If you are not Native American, do not offer to burn sage over the individual.

There are cases when the patient or other person you are ministering to may want to be baptized, be given Communion, or request another type of specific religious ritual. Let them know if you are not part of their faith group. But if another minister is not available and you are able and willing to assist them, then make sure they know that your assistance will not be in an official capacity for their faith tradition. If they or their family members permit you to go ahead and administer that religious practice, then most organizations with chaplaincy departments have policy and positions that it is okay for you to do so. Full disclosure is key in these emergent situations. Just make sure all parties are aware.

9. Use Theological Reflections as Appropriate

Connecting what you hear from the person's story to a theological principle or narrative can be very powerful and moving for the person in need. This helps keep the conversation of the encounter spiritual and not simply social in nature. As the conversation becomes emotional and spiritual, the chaplain may mention the interjection of a theological reflection. A theological reflection is sharing with the hurting individual an appropriate scriptural or theological parallel that may reflect the situation and give the individual emotional and spiritual support. These analogies open up conversation and allow patients an opportunity to begin expressing their faith and what gives them strength or not in the midst of their crises. For example, if you are speaking to someone who seems to have everything in the world going against them, the biblical narrative of Job would be appropriate. I would not stop and interject a ten-to-fifteen-minute sermonette on Job to them, but I would restate the obvious struggles of Job in view of the current situation.

For the Christian chaplain, this gives the patient room to think and explore his or her own situation and whether a theological understanding will help them cope better. It also allows the power of the Holy Spirit to work in their lives, stimulate deeper spiritual concerns, and pave the way for salvation.

Of course, use an appropriate theological reflection. I would not assume that a Muslim police officer or a Hindu coworker would fully understand the "Christian" phrase and symbolism of "the thorn in Peter's side." Theological reflections are most helpful when based upon the other person's faith and spiritual tradition. Gaining a better understanding of diverse expressions of the world faiths and spirituality can be another great skill. More time and discussion of understanding diverse faith and spirituality expressions will be in another volume of this skill set series.

10. Speak Slower than Normal, Maintain Good Eye Contact, and Use Good Situational Awareness

These ministry principles are fundamental. As you know, when people are stressed, they are not able to concentrate on what you are saying very well. Speaking fast will not help, and it may actually create even more stress and confusion. Speak slower—but not in a way that could be received as insulting. Provide brief pauses between comments to observe if the other person is mentally tracking with you. Eye contact is important as well, but be aware of whether it is culturally appropriate to do so or not. Also, be situationally aware. Observe the behavior of other people who may be present. Do they need assistance as well? Do you need to take the one you are ministering to another location for more privacy? If so, keep appropriate professional boundaries. It is usually best to remain visible to others so that any outbursts and behaviors can be witnessed. Doing so will protect you from any misunderstandings of physical touch and sexual advances. Keep it professional, chaplains!

11. Understand Empathy versus Sympathy

Sympathy is widely defined as having feelings of pity and sorrow for someone else's situation or misfortune that you care and are sorry about his or her troubles. But sympathy is often expressed in ways that tend to lighten the mood of the situation. *Empathy* is defined as having the capacity to understand, identity with, and project your known emotions into the situation of another person's similar experiences and emotions.

Brene' Brown's research in this area observed that empathy rarely starts with the words, "At least." Oftentimes, the best response is "I don't know what to say, but I am really glad you told me." Brown pays tribute to nursing scholar Theresa Wiseman's four attributes of empathy. Wiseman defines empathy as:

1. To be able to see the world as others see it.
2. To be nonjudgmental and not discount another person's experience or emotions.
3. To understand another person's feelings, we have to be in touch with our own feelings and emotions in order to truly understand theirs.
4. To communicate your understanding of that person's feelings.

Try not to use phrases like "At least you" or "It could be worse." These phrases minimize and discount the other person's emotions and experiences. In times of crisis, it is not appropriate to tell them to "move on" or "get over it," or say, "It is really not that bad, is it?" Brene' Brown has conducted great research and written several great texts on this. All chaplains should read it for their own emotional health first, which will allow them to be able to assist others in greater depth.[18] Chaplains, learn to show true empathy.

---

[18] Brene' Brown, *The Gifts of Imperfection*. Center City: Hazelden, 2010. Other works by Brown include *I Thought It was Just Me (But It Isn't)* (New York: Gotham Books, 2007) and *Daring Greatly: How the Courage to Be Vulnerable Transforms the Way We Live, Love, Parent, and Lead.* (New York: Gotham Books, (2012).

12. Do Not Overfunction

Often, less is best—in doing and in speaking. Use your intuition. Your calm presence in the midst of crisis and chaos will be respected and recognized even if you do not feel that you are doing much at all. Being there is doing something. Before an encounter, I often simply say a quiet prayer to myself for the Holy Spirit to guide my interactions and conversations when I am called to be present at a trauma situation. Often, I am simply led to just "be" while being respectful to all parties. I often serve them by remaining very patient as I slowly foster conversations to help process difficult emotions. During this type of encounter, the chaplain's sensitivity, patience, empathy, and intuition are extremely important.

13. Other Needed Skill Sets

Death Notification Protocols

Understanding simple yet quality techniques of proper death notifications is paramount for effective chaplains. Deaths occur, and chaplains are called upon to assist in notifying loved ones. The information presented here is based upon Kenneth V. Iserson's work.[19] Iserson's basic four-step protocol of *prepare, inform, support,* and *afterward* will be taught and discussed. It is recommended that any direct theological questions from patient families to a health-care service provider should be politely referred to a chaplain or a patient's own minister(s) for appropriate follow-up.

Prepare (Anticipate, Identify, and Notify)

Begin by *anticipating* what needs are required for the situation. Normally, a private place to talk and a place to sit comfortably are needed. Various types of deaths may require different approaches.

---

[19] Kenneth V. Iserson, *Pocket Protocols: Notifying Survivors about Sudden, Unexpected Deaths* (Tucson: Galen Press, Ltd., 1999).

These variations will be discussed. Be certain to *identify* the survivors. Is everyone who needs to know present—or should you wait a few minutes longer for others to arrive? If you cannot be certain of the decedent's identity, say so immediately. Find out what relatives already know before saying more. If the patient is dying or resuscitation is continuing, *inform* survivors of the severity of the situation and the patient's critical physical condition. During the resuscitation, update them regularly. Make sure that you arrange enough time to speak with survivors without feeling or being perceived as rushed.

Inform (Identify and Tell)

Always introduce yourself and those accompanying you. Use clear, nontechnical language. If the decedent's identity is still in question after death, two options are to describe the decedent or to take a photo of their cleaned face only and then share with a member of the group. Use a D word such as "*died*," "*death*," or "*dead*." Then pause and allow the survivors to grasp the meaning of those words and emotionally react. Never apologize for the death. Listen if relatives want to talk or ask questions. Be very respectful and professional. Explain details when asked and what they may expect to see if they choose to view the decedent after the decedent is cleaned up and prepared for viewing.

Support (Reassure, Relieve, Assist, and Conclude)

Reassure the survivors that all medical options were made to resuscitate and care for the patient. Provide the survivors relief in knowing that their family member or friend did not suffer. If the death occurred during an accident or at the hand of another, do your best to help remove any family guilt or mental anguish. *Assist* survivors with continued privacy, protect them from media (if present), and help make pertinent phone contacts. *Assist* with helping arrange transportation and overnight accommodations if needed. *Assist* in deciding about funeral arrangements, medical interviews with coroner, and organ or tissue donations. *Conclude* by asking survivors if they have further questions or concerns that you may help them. Accompany survivors to the exit while providing emotional and spiritual support as appropriate for situation.

Afterward (Debrief and Follow Up)

Notify staff that they can release information about the death to appropriate callers once family is notified. If it warrants, schedule any operational or emotional stress debriefings for staff. *Follow up* with a sympathy card or letter of condolences to family and friends through your department or chaplain's office. If bereavement services are available, inform survivors of the time and place the services will be held.

PART 2

Understanding Spirituality and World Faith Expressions

CHAPTER 5

The Need

I am a clinical hospital chaplain. You might also consider me a workplace (or marketplace/corporate) chaplain. I say that because I work with patients and families, and I also spend a great deal of time building relationships with the organization's employees in order to minister to them as needs arise. My doctoral work centered on a ministry-development project evaluating a specific workplace spirituality environment. The objective was to discover if there were new initiatives that could be implemented to improve the workplace spirituality perception as well as the practical application of spirituality with employees. I will discuss the spiritual assessment of individuals and organizations later in this text.

It did not take long into my literature review and research endeavor to realize that I did not have enough experience with diverse world faiths. I did not truly understand how different faiths and belief systems expressed themselves (verbally and nonverbally) or how different beliefs guide daily decision making and a person's perspective of hope, inner peace, and life satisfaction. I needed to brush up on my understanding of spirituality expressions, and I needed to do it quickly. I asked myself, "How can chaplains serving any workplace function to their greatest potential? How can chaplains achieve the best outcomes for their organization? Can this occur if the chaplain does not understand the spirituality and faith demographics of those he or she ministers?" This was where I found myself: responsible but not being held accountable.

Yes, chaplains can do a quality assessment and encounter without any pre-knowledge of the people they are speaking with, but if they possess a good understanding of the diverse world faiths and the way each is expressed, it can demonstrate greater professionalism, reduce the chaplain's possible anxiety and any awkward moments with a more positive result of engaging in deeper spiritual conversation with the patient or worker. This section will help chaplains of all styles and life experiences become more intentional in their conversations as well as in their spiritual assessments.

Most chaplains operate on the assumption that spirituality exists and every person possesses a spirituality—whether they fully recognize it or not.[20] But one's spirituality is not by nature or by definition solely about religion or religiosity. This principle has become a foundational pillar for my chaplaincy. Judith A. Neal states that most management authors and consultants in the field of workplace spirituality:

> Define the human being as consisting of four parts or four types of energy: (1) Physical: Our ability to take good care of our bodies and physical well-being; (2) Mental: Our ability to think clearly, learn, and make good decisions; (3) Emotional: Our ability to create positive relationships and to handle difficult situations; (4) Spiritual: Our ability to connect to something greater than ourselves and to be of service in the world.[21]

---

[20] Joan Marques, Dhiman Satinder, and Richard King, *Spirituality in the Workplace: What It Is, Why It Matters, How To Make It Work For You* (Fawnskin: Personhood Press, 2007), 6–7.

[21] Judith A. Neal, "Spirituality in the Workplace." accessed May 22, 2014, http://judineal.com/pages/pubs/academic1.htm#spirit.

Gilbert Fairholm adds,

> One's spirituality is the essence of who he or she is. It defines the inner self, separate from the body, but including the physical and intellectual self [...] Spirituality also is the quality of being spiritual, of recognizing the intangible, life-affirming force in self and all human beings. It is a state of intimate relationship with the inner self of higher values and morality. It is recognition of the truth of the inner nature of people.[22]

Science can tell us how something functions, but it does not tell us why or its motivations. I strongly feel that spirituality, faith, and moral beliefs guide all of our choices and motivations. As French Jesuit priest, paleontologist, and philosopher Pierre Teilhard de Chardin acclaimed, "We are not human beings having a spiritual experience; we are spiritual beings having a human experience." I will not discuss the theology or doctrine behind this statement, but it does relate that all humans have a choice to look well beyond their physical existence for life's purpose and meaning. Our worldview of spirituality and faith definitely informs and shapes each of our perspectives.

For scholars, it has taken many years to arrive at a consensus on how to define spirituality since spirituality can be viewed from many perspectives. Christina Puchalski, MD, serves as the director of the George Washington Institute of Spirituality and Health. In 2009 and 2014, Puchalski moderated a health-care panel for spirituality and palliative care and assisted in producing a consensus definition for spirituality. The panel concluded: "Spirituality is the aspect of humanity that refers to the way individuals seek and express meaning and purpose and the way they experience their connectedness to the moment, to self, to others, to nature, and to the significant or sacred."[23]

---

[22] Gilbert Fairholm, *Capturing the Heart of Leadership: Spirituality and Community in the New American Workplace* (Westport: Praeger Publishers, 1997), 29. Accessed July 29, 2014. http://books.google.com.

[23] Puchalski (2014), 642.

Others perceive that spirituality stems from one's inner consciousness and is the source behind the outward form of defined religious practices.[24] Religion is more strictly defined as how one's spirituality is practiced within a specific doctrinal or theological context. In a white paper on professional chaplaincy, spirituality is explained as "an awareness of relationships with all creation, an appreciation of presence and purpose that includes a sense of meaning. Though not true generations ago, a distinction is frequently made today between spirituality and religion, the latter focusing on defined structures, rituals and doctrines. While religion and medicine were virtually inseparable for thousands of years, the advent of science created a chasm between the two. The term spirituality is a contemporary bridge that renews this relationship."[25]

Studies of the spiritual paradigm repeatedly reveal that "people not only work with their hands, but also their hearts and spirit."[26] Louis Fry's research of spiritual business leadership observed that when workers' inner lives are able to consistently fuel hope and faith into a more transcendent vision of service in all parts of their life, they will begin to live life as it was created—as a precious gift.[27] A problem that many chaplains possess is understanding the myriad ways spirituality and diverse faith traditions are personally expressed and how it is later manifested in many ways throughout the individual's life, including his or her work life.

An individual's spirituality shapes his or her perspective on life and level of future hope. This is key to possessing realistic optimism and governs daily resiliency in distress or crises. Due to this principle, I will address whether or not each faith believes in a spiritual afterlife and what the path of salvation for each demands.

---

[24] Guillory, xi.
[25] VandeCreek and Burton (2001), 82.
[26] Pawinee Petchsawanga and Dennis Duchon, "Workplace Spirituality, Meditation, and Work Performance." *Journal of Management, Spirituality and Religion* 9, no. 2 (June 2012): 190.
[27] Louis W. Fry and Melissa Sadler Nisiewicz, *Maximizing the Triple Bottom Line through Spiritual Leadership* (Stanford: Stanford Business Books, 2013), Kindle eBook Location 1096–1116.

Three Main Worldviews

Worldview and culture experts place an individual's view of God or ultimate reality into several general categories based upon whether ultimate reality is knowable or not.[28] The most basic categories are naturalism, transcendentalism, and theism.

> *Naturalism* includes those worldviews that suggest ultimate reality is limited to the physical matter of the universe; *transcendentalism* includes those that see ultimate reality as being only spiritual or physic (mental energy); and *theism* refers to those worldviews that posit a personal God as ultimate reality who created the material and spiritual universe.[29]

Naturalism

In a nutshell, naturalism cites that all things are merely physical in nature. For naturalism, there is no God or spiritual afterlife. Once life ceases, that is it. Naturalists do not believe that there is any force or God that is greater or beyond ourselves to give our lives deeper meaning or purpose.

If a person holds to the worldview of naturalism—there is nothing beyond or separate from that which they can see, touch, and/or measure. Matter and energy are the basic "stuff" from which all existence is derived. Such a view of reality implies that all obtainable answers for "the ultimate questions" relating to the universe and mankind can be found by the investigation of the physical world.

Various ideas that stem from naturalism are materialism, positivism, secularism, scientism, atheism, and agnosticism. These ideas are expressed as secular humanism, Marxism/Leninism (i.e. socialism), existentialism, nihilism, and hedonism.[30]

---

[28] W. Gary Phillips, William E. Brown, and John Stonestreet, *Making Sense of Your World: A Biblical Worldview* (Salem, WI: Sheffield Publishing, 2008), 22–23.
[29] Phillips et al, 22.
[30] Phillips et al.

For contrast, if the Christian Bible says, "In the beginning, God …" the naturalist mindset would want to reword this by saying, "In the beginning, hydrogen." In naturalism, the supernatural God is replaced by natural elements, so if there are no spiritual realities, then it is impossible for God to exist. For the naturalist, reality is understood only by the careful use of the scientific method, not wishful thinking (as they view creationists and Christians).

Science had tenaciously held to a belief in God as the conclusion that the orderly physical properties of earth (i.e. gravity) served as a constant proof of an orderly God. Up until that point, "All truth was God's truth," and the starry heavens above blinked down God's favor upon a grateful people. All that began to change in the eighteenth and nineteenth centuries. Now science tries to avoid any premise that God is a factor at all in their theories.

Transcendentalism

The second general worldview category is transcendentalism. Transcendentalism sees all of life and the universe as spiritual in nature. Prime reality or ultimate reality is the force that is all around and within us. Transcendentalists believe that all of life as well as inanimate objects are part God and interconnected. Transcendentalism views that humanity is God. Transcendentalism sees the world as you want it to be. Ideas of Transcendentalism are seen in pantheism, panentheism, polytheism, animism, panpsychism, and new age. Transcendentalism is described as "a melting pot of mystical and psychic movements."[31] Expressions of transcendentalism are: Buddhism, Hinduism, Taoism, Confucianism, Hare Krishna, Baha'ism, new age beliefs, Scientology and Wicca.

Transcendentalism promises a progression toward universal unity. Modern society is enamored with the concept of progression. Who wouldn't like a belief that the world is ultimately moving toward global unity? That's a much better solution than a biblical

---

[31] Phillips et al, 33.

Armageddon. The most positive aspect of transcendentalism is the promise of a "new age" of global harmony and peace. However, scholars observe, "As mankind progresses toward this unity, the shackles of theistic religions and atheistic naturalism must be removed."[32] In a nutshell, transcendentalism views that man is God. Transcendentalism "replaces the Theistic view of man's depravity with a positive acclamation of man's own divinity."[33] This perspective intertwines well "with an American culture that prides itself on individual determination and accomplishment. Actualizing one's divine nature results in breakthrough experiences for individuals in their careers, health, and relationships."[34]

Theism

The third main worldview is Theism. Theism sees the world from God's hands. Theism can look to many gods (polytheism) or toward one god (monotheism). We will quickly delve into the worldview of monotheism, whether the God is only distant or extremely relational, personal, and engaging. Expressions of Theism are Islam, Judaism, and biblical Christianity.

Surveys have noted that three-fifths of our world population believes there is a personal deity.[35] While naturalism builds its system on the assumption that the material universe is all there is; transcendentalism assumes that all reality is of one great mind or spirit. Theism begins with the assumption that God exists.

Judaism believes in one God—but not that Christ the Messiah has returned. Islam believes in one God, Allah, but this is not Christianity's triune God that is comprised of God the Father, God the Son, and God the Spirit. One should not say that all faiths lead to heaven and to the same Creator Lord, but many do. That premise

---

[32] Phillips et al, 38.
[33] Phillips et al, 38.
[34] Phillips et al.
[35] D. Barrett, *World Christian Encyclopedia,* 2nd ed., (New York: Oxford, 2001).

may help everyone feel good, but that is not theologically correct per the Torah, the Holy Bible, and the Qu'ran.

Theism holds that real things do exist beyond the physical realm: God, angels, the human soul, immortality, and the like. Christianity speaks of eternal things not seen, which naturalism cannot and even avoids (Genesis 1:1; 2 Corinthians 4:17; Hebrews 11:1). Theism sees the created world as a work of art from the hand of the Creator. Christian theism also delivers an indictment against man because of his personal rebellion against the truth revealed by God.

Discerning a Worldview

Professor and historian Glenn Sunshine has written several texts regarding worldview and world faiths. I highly recommend his texts for chaplains who desire to study deeper on this topic. Instead of the three primary worldviews as presented above, Sunshine expands upon these three to include several more variations. In his text *Portals: Entering Your Neighbor's World*, Sunshine divides his worldview discussion into seven categories: historic Christianity, secular naturalism, postmodernism, Islam, Eastern religions, new age movement, and the Gaian worldview.[36]

But how does a spiritual care provider discern which worldview an individual may possess? In Sunshine's text, he evaluates worldviews by the answers to four fundamental questions of life:

(1) Where did I come from?
(2) What is wrong with the world?
(3) Is there a solution?
(4) What is my purpose?

---

[36] Glenn Sunshine, *Portals: Entering Your Neighbor's World*, (Newington, CT: Every Square Inch Publishing, 2012). Another great work by Glenn Sunshine is *Why You Think the Way You Do* (Zondervan, 2009).

In *The Universe Next Door*, James Sire relates that each worldview can be expressed in propositions to seven basic questions:

(1) What is prime reality?
(2) What is the nature of external reality, that is, the world around us?
(3) What is a human being?
(4) What happens to a person at death?
(5) Why is it possible to know anything at all?
(6) How do we know what is right and wrong?
(7) What is the meaning of human history?[37]

There are many other philosophers who pose various questions of life, but these listed by Sunshine and Sire are at the core and are useful for chaplains to consider personally as well as during their conversations.

Phillips, Brown, and Stonestreet assert that each individual's theological worldview must try to answer the ultimate questions of life. These questions are placed in the following categories:

- *Origins of Life*: Why am I alive? What is the cause of my existence? Why are humans here? Are humans different or superior to other life? Why?
- *Identity*: Who am I? What is humanity? What does it mean to be human? How do I fit in with the world?
- *Meaning and Purpose*: Why am I here? Why should man be concerned with education, social justice issues, stewardship of earth resources, family values, etc.?

---

[37] James W. Sire, *The Universe Next Door: A Basic Worldview Catalog*, Fifth ed., (Downers Grove, IL: IVP Academic, 2009), 22–23.

- *Morality/Destiny*: Is there a right or wrong? How am I supposed to live and behave? If there is a moral code, what is it based upon? Should morality be absolute or relative?
- *Mortality*: What happens when I die? What really is my spirit or soul? Is there life after death? If so, what happens after death and what determines what happens?

Worldview	Origin	Identity	Meaning	Morality	Destiny
Naturalism	Natural causes and processes	Self-conscious animals	No source for ultimate meaning	Human-centered (relative)	No afterlife, no ultimate direction to history
Transcendentalism	Fragmentation of divine oneness	Expression of divine oneness	Seek unity with all things	Human-centered (relative)	All people and things return to divine oneness
Theism	Created by God	Special creation of God	Determined by God for His creation	God-centered (absolute)	Eternal life (with or apart from God)

Table 1: Three Primary Worldviews
(Phillips, Brown, and Stonestreet, 2008, 40)

To begin to understand this more fully, chapters 6 through 11 will outline the general faith doctrine and the spirituality expressions from each of these primary categories. Chapter 6 will review the naturalistic expression of humanism. Chapters 7 and 8 will review the transcendental expressions of Buddhist spirituality and Hindu spirituality, respectively. Chapters 9, 10, and 11 will review the theistic spiritual expressions of Islam, Judaism, and Christianity. The goal of this systematic review is to provide broader understanding of the core beliefs and physical expressions of each belief system, thereby allowing for an indirect comparison of these primary world faiths.

The reader is encouraged to delve deeper into each—as well as the hundreds and hundreds of "minor" religions and faiths that are present in our diverse world. Following this section on review spirituality expressions, the *Essential Chaplain Skill Sets* will discuss how to conduct individual spiritual assessments and evaluate an organization or group's spirituality.

CHAPTER 6

Spirituality of Humanism

There are many viewpoints of what spirituality should be and should not be. Due to the large content of information, I need to be general and basic in description. In this section, Unitarian Universalist Rev. Kee and I will lay out some theoretical concepts of spirituality and humanism. This will be followed by a discussion between us that will express her specific views of secular and religious humanism as well as how her spirituality has meaning in her life and is practically expressed. This should be particularly helpful for ministers and chaplains of all faith traditions and settings.

The general concept of spirituality is stated to be humanistic in nature by humanist David Elkins, but it is also expressed differently through the various lenses of faith. Devoid of any theological language, the Washington Ethical Society (www.ethicalsociety.org) defines,

> Humanistic spirituality is experiencing ourselves as vitally connected to other human beings, to nature, and the universe. Spirituality means respecting spiritual well-being as deserving special attention, not to be trivialized or violated. As we travel through the stages of life from birth to death, we learn to create satisfying relationships with people, nature, and the universe, or we suffer the consequences.

From a psychological perspective, one literature review on humanistic spirituality supports the perspectives of Erich Fromm, Carl Jung, and Viktor Frankl that concern for the soul does not have to be specifically religious in nature. In fact, minister-turned-humanist David N. Elkins relates that Carl Jung was only able to cure those who had recovered a spiritual orientation for life.[38] Regarding this humanism perspective of spirituality, one group states,

> This is not an anti-religion stance. In our view a humanistic approach to spirituality is not an attempt to invalidate religion … A humanistic approach to spirituality is at variance only with narrow religion that would claim a monopoly on spirituality and would refuse to recognize its human and universal nature.[39]

The Elkins study identifies nine distinct components for humanistic spirituality:

- There is an experientially based belief in a transcendent dimension.
- There is a sense and a deep quest that all of life has a deeper meaning and purpose.
- The spiritual individual possesses a sense of mission or vocation for life that immerses all of life's goals and activities.
- There is a sacredness of life that exists in which a sense of awe, reverence, and wonder even in nonreligious settings perfuses all of life.
- Materialism is not viewed as a goal for ultimate satisfaction.
- Altruistic love and action are at the core in guiding social justice and assisting others in suffering and pain.

---

[38] David N. Elkins, L. James Hedstrom, Lori L. Hughes, J. Andrew Leaf, and Cheryl Saunders, "Toward a Humanistic-Phenomenological Spirituality: Definition, Description, and measurement" *Journal of Humanistic Psychology* 28, no. 5 (1988): 7.

[39] Elkins, 8.

- There is an idealism and a vision toward the betterment of the world. The spirituality of the humanist sees the greater potential for what things may become.
- There is the awareness of the reality of human suffering, pain, and global tragedy, which provides an existential seriousness for the humanist.
- There is the awareness that spirituality has added a discernible effect or "fruit" to his or her life.

The researchers of this study conclude, "[a]n enlarged, humanistic approach to Spirituality, however, offers an opportunity to study the spirituality … in a more sensitive manner."[40] On counterpoint, these same nine components could easily be used to describe any of the primary world faiths. The arguable difference would be where or upon what is the focus and intention of the individual. Spirituality can be manifested either inwardly for self-help only or externally in recognition and worship of a Creator God.

As Rev. Kee will confirm, the concept of spirituality is multifaceted. Everyone embodies a spirituality that is expressed and utilized in many ways. The focus may be upon self-transcendence and personal transformation. This may or may not include an understanding of an external deity.

The spiritual nature of the human being involves the capacity to transcend our own sense of self and therefore gain an appreciation or even blending with an imminent divine. Spirituality may also mean a connectedness with nature and the cosmos. For example, Thoreau and Emerson's poetry captures this capacity for transcendence, especially when a person experiences "a sense of awe and wonder" in nature since nature can be a primary initiator. Other experiences like a birth of a child, a work of art or music, an act of grace or extreme kindness are also examples that often trigger a transcendent moment in life. A genuine and well-balanced spirituality is said to

---

[40] Elkins, 16.

Essential Chaplain Skill Sets

manifest in deeper inner awareness, personal peace, and freedom of the individual.[41]

Much of past difficulty in defining spirituality stems from the notions of how the terms *spirit* and *spiritual* are understood. George Saint-Laurent observes that the word *spirit,* whether figuratively or literally, is ordinarily used "to express a dimension of our experience that is nonphysical and inaccessible to the senses."[42] This is often expressed as someone possesses a *spirit* of courageousness, gentleness, or compassion. The word *spirit* is also commonly interchanged as a synonym for soul: however, the theological nuances of an individual's spirit and soul will not be discussed here. Saint-Laurent states,

> Our spirit is the immaterial and immortal ground within us for all our mental and volitional activities, not only for our encounter with God or the Godhead but also for our relatedness to other human beings. From this perspective, our spirit is a non-corporeal entity that not only animates us but also empowers us for specifically human consciousness and activity.[43]

To restate, the human spirit is the nonphysical or non-corporeal component of life that gives humanity personhood. The adjective form of spirit is *spiritual* when used to "highlight a nonphysical yet significantly human quality" or when applied "to experiences, things, and places." With regard to the human spirit or one's spirituality, the concern is an important part of personhood as its focus is toward the inner meaning of experiences and how experiences impact the individual's worldview of life, purpose and meaning, and decision-making.[44] Even if one does not affirm the existence of a spiritual soul,

---

[41] George E. Saint-Laurent, *Spirituality and World Religions: A Comparative Introduction* (Mountain View: Mayfield Publishing Co, 2000), 3.
[42] Saint-Laurent, 4.
[43] Saint-Laurent, 5.
[44] Saint-Laurent, 6–14.

as the Buddhists deny, one's spirituality is still "a dimension that directs the flow of consciousness and characterizes" one's actions.[45]

With this context for a broad understanding of spirituality as an experiential and transformational process, it is also important to understand the various nuances of how spirituality is perceived within the primary world religions. Religion can be viewed as the particular way one's spirituality is displayed and practiced based upon a certain doctrine and theology. Religion can also be viewed as a pursuit or quest toward personal significance, transformation, and purpose.

Most world religions teach that deep inner peace and the meaning of life come from a source beyond this earthly world as one humbly seeks satisfying answers to humanity's most complex questions. Whether the decided path to follow is the Jewish "way of Torah," the Christian "the way" (*hodos*), the Muslim "straight path" (*shariah*), the Hindu four major "ways" (*margas*) to liberation, or the Buddhist "middle way" (*magga*) to enlightenment. The intent of the seeker is to journey toward a deeper personal transformation of the spiritual self.[46]

For Jews, Christians, and Muslims, this personal transformation requires atonement of humanity's primary problem—sin. This premise is seen throughout the Qur'an and the Holy Bible:

> "Indeed, Allah does not forgive association with Him, but He forgives what is less than that for whom He wills. And he who associates others with Allah has certainly gone far astray."
> —Qur'an, Sūrah an-Nisā, "The Women" 4:116
>
> "If my people who are called by my name will humble themselves, and pray and seek my face, and turn from their wicked ways, then I will hear from heaven and will forgive their sin and heal their land."
> —Holy Bible, 2 Chronicles 7:14 (ESV)

---

[45] Saint-Laurent, 7.
[46] Saint-Laurent, 23.

"Except for those who repent, believe and do righteous work. For them Allah will replace their evil deeds with good. And ever is Allah Forgiving and Merciful."
—Qur'an, Sūrah al-Furqān "The Criterion" 25:70

"For God so loved the world that He gave his only Son, that whoever believes in him should not perish but have eternal life."
—Holy Bible, John 3:16 (ESV)

"Say, 'O My servants who have transgressed against themselves [by sinning], do not despair of the mercy of Allah. Indeed, Allah forgives all sins. Indeed, it is He who is the Forgiving, the Merciful.'"
—Qur'an, Sūrah az-Zumar, "The Groups" 39:53.

"For all have sinned and fall short of the glory of God."
—Holy Bible, Romans 3:23 (ESV)

"For the wages of sin is death, but the free gift of God is eternal life in Christ Jesus our Lord."
—Holy Bible, Romans 6:23 (ESV)

For Jews and Christians, atonement comes from a benevolent God. For Muslims, atonement is achieved from personal actions. For Hindus and Buddhists, the primary problem of mankind is not sin but intellectual blindness as "human beings erroneously fail to see things for what they really are, and become trapped by the law of karma ... on the wheel of endless rebirth."[47] I realize that this may be a sweeping generalization of the groups and that many nuances and differences do exist in the manner in which individuals perceive, experience, and practice their spirituality.

All five of the major world religions see the primary problem of humanity as stemming from a deficit of the "self." One's view or theology of mankind (i.e., doctrines of anthropology) propagates

---

[47] Saint-Laurent, 24.

the varied differences. When one refers to the Abrahamic religions, there is a "problem of humanity" through the doctrine of original sin. Many smaller religions do not have a vertical hierarchical structure with an anthropomorphized deity at the top. Many traditions have humans as part of the natural world/creation, and that which is divine is an ongoing process of revelation. Based upon the religious tradition, humans may not be viewed as inherently good or bad: they are simply participants in the web of life and the natural world.

The dramatic differences between the primary religions are the process and pursuit of identifying, reducing, and/or removing "self" and how inner joy and peace is achieved. From the humanist standpoint, it could be stated that the "whole self" is the starting point. I interviewed humanist Leslie Kee for her perspectives.

Rev. Kee: First, humanism should not be categorized as a religion: it is a philosophy. Second, an individual who self-identifies as a humanist will often preclude statements with some sort of disclaimer that states she/he does not speak on behalf of all humanists, only themselves, which I find to be an agreeable form of individualism.

Because I self-identify as a humanist, my philosophy is grounded in the belief that human beings are spiritual by nature, which is also constitutive to each person's inherent worth and dignity. As a humanist, I reject the doctrine of original sin and the redemption of sin as put forth by the Christian doctrine of Jesus's death of atonement. Rather, I agree with the feminist scholars, in particular Luce Irigaray and Grace Jantzen, who put forth a theory of *natalities*, which shifts fundamental religious imagery from death and suffering to natality (birth and the flourishing of life).

As a humanist, for me, the spiritual and religious experiences are not about removing the self in the Freudian ego sense: rather, the self is an "I am me" holistic understanding. From birth, my growing awareness of myself is based on my inherent physiological, rational, and intuitive capabilities. I understand this set of capabilities to be a fundamental attribute of our true human nature, which is then reflected back to me through the various relationships that define my life.

The religious and spiritual impulse is about making sense and meaning throughout the processes of living. I believe there is no predestined plan created by a deity and no karmic wheel spinning through reincarnated lifetimes. Instead, I understand myself to be an active participant in the cycle of birth, life, and death. The purpose of my life is to use my capacity for reason, compassion, love, forgiveness, awe, imagination, and inspiration to be the best human I can while living within my own individuality as well as within a community of relationships.

I self-identify as a religious humanist because I find value in religious community. For me, religious community is a physical place for like-minded folks to gather for the purpose of intellectual exchange and stimulation; for bringing difficult moral, ethical, and theological questions; for exploring many different sources in the quest for answers; for affirmation of our basic humanity; for forgiveness; and for ritualized celebrations such as marriage, death, and birth. For me, observance of all of the above, plus a healthy dose of Mother Nature, are a large part of what constitutes my philosophy of religion.

It is my understanding that someone who self-identifies as a secular humanist is not drawn to a religious community in the same way I am. Rather, this person is perhaps more comfortable finding meaning in a less "religiously traditional" setting.

I always make an important clarification on behalf of all of us who self-identify as humanist: just because you don't believe in a deity, particularly an "Our Father in heaven" deity doesn't mean you don't believe in anything. As spiritual beings, humans are hardwired to believe, period. This speaks to the capacity for transcendence—to be awed, to be humbled, to have our perspectives challenged and inspired by that which is larger than the individual self.

Too many people accuse humanists of "worshipping" humans (i.e., putting themselves on par or above God.) This is not true. It is more accurate to say that humanists are realists when it comes to what it means to be human. Humanist philosophy grounds being human in our innate capabilities to serve that which causes life to flourish here on earth. I do not know many fellow humanists who think human beings are perfect, but I think we share a belief in our tremendous capacity to use our innate capabilities to serve a common good. But because we are human, we tend to be our own worst enemies (falling for false idols, succumbing to the easy way, or losing sight of the power of love instead of fear).

As I've grown older, I believe more strongly than ever that the doctrine of original sin is still doing substantial damage to our collective psyche. When you drill it into your children, by their very nature sinful and bad, they will either live up to this expectation or have a miserable time trying to unlearn it and discover their true nature. If you tell a child she/he is smart, good, imaginative, and capable of learning from her/his mistakes, you have a whole different set of expectations—more, healthy, realistic, and humane.

Also, I believe the doctrine of third-party atonement is very disempowering. It just doesn't make sense that a human being was put to death over two thousand years ago to forgive my sins. If I do something that needs forgiving, it is my responsibility to seek forgiveness from the one I hurt and especially forgiveness of myself. No one can atone for me, just like no one can be born for me or die for me. Teaching generations of children they are first and foremost sinful creatures and then not being able to atone for their own mistakes is just plain bad psychology.

As for eschatology, humanist philosophy posits that whether or not there is an afterlife is not the issue: instead, it is possible to live this life as an ethical human being. Humanists believe it is perfectly fine to be good just for the sake of being good. Because we are fundamentally loving beings born with spiritual integrity, if we are good and there is a heaven, we will go to it—if there isn't, then we won't—but there is no way to prove the existence or nonexistence of this place. It is more important to live this life lovingly with integrity and to the best of our ability.

What are some helpful ways that a chaplain can better engage a humanistic patient to discuss spirituality and beliefs?

Kee: I have never heard a person whose beliefs fall within the philosophy of humanism referred to as humanistic. It is an adjectival form that seems awkward. The term *humanist* is the most common usage. We also meet folks who self-identify as humanists but who specify their beliefs further as religious humanists or a secular humanists.

Many people who do not adhere to a traditional religion tend not to label themselves as humanist since humanism is not a religion. But if a chaplain is referencing a set of boxed check marks on an admission form, then the conversation would probably be taking place with someone who checked "none."

Therefore, I always start by asking, "How are you?" Once we move through the clinical answers and I have a sense of this person's emotional state, I follow their lead in the conversation. In general, I might say, "There is a lot going on in your life right now. How are you doing? I see your head has it figured out. How is your heart doing?"

As the discussion moves along, active listening is essential, especially as a sincere reflection of what the person is saying while paying attention to emotional nuances. If they seem to be struggling spiritually (i.e., seeking meaning in what is happening and why, or perhaps an internal peace), I try to get them to talk about their struggle. "Do you have a faith tradition? Why or why not?" Once they begin to share, I continue to reflect and ask open-ended questions. Depending on the person, some of my questions are direct ("Do you believe in God?") or indirect ("Have you ever had what you thought was a spiritual experience? What was growing up like? Did your parents take you to a church?" Again, good listening skills are essential.

From a humanist perspective, there is a core belief that each person is capable of answering his or her own questions adequately, but I frequently discover past experiences with organized religions and their associated doctrines are what most often get in the way of spiritual clarity. Often, especially in situations of acute spiritual crisis, I find someone who is worried about the supposed ramifications of questioning the nature of God, the existence of God, or shame, guilt, fear, or forgiveness. Traditionally, these are the "religious" subjects that humans wrestle with and whose answers have been generated through organized religions. For a humanist, the subjects are the same, but the sources for answers tend to be more multidimensional and, in many instances, relative.

Once we have established a rapport, I strive to remain mindful of the fact that each encounter is different and, as a chaplain, I should respond accordingly. So, for example, sometimes my responses draw upon my personal experience and study of Buddhism, Native American/earth-based philosophies, psychology, women's spirituality, or my own growth out of Christianity and into religious humanism.

Because I consider myself a spiritual being, I believe good pastoral care begins with an open mind and a "good heart" so a safe spiritual space can be created between the two of us. It is important this spiritual space not be cluttered with anticipation of an outcome, such as a petitionary prayer, a reunion with a deity, or a confession of sin and regret. Instead, I consider my chaplaincy work effective if a shared understanding emerges from within any given encounter—a kind of harmony that we both recognize in each other's eyes and feel with our hearts. My experience of these spiritual moments is very poignant because they are real and mutual—from human to human.

What are some cautions or non-helpful ways for chaplains to be aware of when ministering to an individual with religious or secular humanism beliefs?

Kee: In my experience, there is a very common and unquestioned assumption among many people that if a person agrees to visit with a chaplain, this person believes in God—which is just not true. Personally, I find this assumption somewhat offensive because it means the other person isn't actually hearing what I am saying to them. Too many theists cannot even begin to imagine that a human being can be good without God.

Just because someone may not believe in a god doesn't mean she/he doesn't believe in anything. For those who want to do chaplaincy well, it is imperative to do the soul work that involves coming to a deep internal place where they fully realize why it's okay for someone not to believe in God. During the trust-building part of any given interaction, it is very easy to recognize disingenuousness. When this happens, for me, the whole encounter becomes diminished, and nothing new can be learned about each other because the old separating patterns fall back into place. The goal of pastoral care—spiritual solace—tends to fall by the wayside when the person in need is not truly being heard, their fundamental humanity recognized, and therefore, mutual respect is not manifest.

Another important awareness is demeanor. Too many religious volunteers and/or professionals come into a room with fixed ideas about the nature of salvation, the power of prayer, and the existence of God. In matters of the spirit, for me, there is a heightened awareness, and if someone does not understand this, it shows. When I meet someone who understands this kind of spiritual awareness, we most always recognize it and allow it to be the framework of the encounter.

As a humanist chaplain, the primary expectation I bring is that, most often, a simple human-to-human connection can be made because I understand myself as bearing witness to the other person's humanity and what they are going through. A compassionate demeanor and active listening are essential tools. Take your cues from the other person, knowing the space you have been invited into only has room for your spirit—not your dogmas. The patient is the subject, I am the object, and the purpose of our encounter is for our spirits to recognize each other, and in so doing, all that is appropriate and necessary will become manifest.

Chaplain Keith Evans

Regarding the spiritual assessment of a humanist, how does the humanist find strength, hope, and resiliency through spirituality when facing life struggles?

Kee: Again, I can't speak on behalf of all humanists because there is no unifying creed, doctrine, or set of sacred rituals in which to seek divine assurance. For myself, I find strength, hope, and resilience through my own spiritual practice. My spiritual practice includes engagement with reason as articulated by philosophers, theologians, and other people whose thoughts and ideas challenge me, educate, and inspire me. I ground a lot of my faith in reason and the products of reason. At the same time, I find immense value in poetry.

For me, those images and stories that are more mythological, fantastical, or miraculous are just that—works of the human imagination to be enjoyed just for what they are. But one aspect of being human that never ceases to fascinate and inspire me is when imagination and ingenuity come together: for example, skyscrapers, bridges, supersonic jets, computers, and cell phones. Human ingenuity is one of the best qualities human beings are born with! I place great faith in it.

The other significant aspect of my humanist spiritual practice is seeking the solace and inspiration that only Mother Nature can provide. In this way, I tell those who ask that I practice an "earth-based spirituality." When I go to the mountains, the prairies, the rivers and lakes, or the oceans, I am humbled, awed, inspired, and strengthened. It is probably fair to say that a significant percentage of others who self-identify as humanists feel the same way about nature. We don't worship it: rather, within it, we find spiritual sustenance.

The other part of how I live my life as a spiritual being is finding the sacred in the mundane. So for me, to engage in things like cooking, cleaning, tending my garden, taking a walk, or getting ready for work, I practice the Buddhist way of mindfulness. In this way, I bring intentionality and meaning to the everyday—nothing is meaningless, and everything has value. I find this outlook has helped keep my life in balance between my blessings and what could become false needs.

What are some common methods that humanists utilize to help them cope, as well as discover deeper purpose, meaning, and satisfaction in life?

Kee: Because humanism is not a religion, there aren't things like ritualized prayer or sacred observances, like Lent or Communion (unless a particular humanist finds comfort in these particular rituals, then go for it!). Instead, faith is placed in the ability of each person to find what it is in life that brings them deeper meaning, a sense of purpose, and satisfaction.

As a minister, I encourage people to create a spiritual practice that fits them and facilitates renewal, a very personal type of contentment, and a sense of spiritual well-being. In this way, the beautiful diversity of humanity is honored—bicycling, baking, camping, reading, gardening, sewing, or making furniture, music, art, dance, writing, prayers, and meditation—all of that which makes up human life becomes a source of spiritual substance because it engages our true human nature, which is fundamentally loving and creative. I believe if each of us lives with awareness, intention, and compassion, then we are behaving as spiritual beings (behaviors that are pleasing to God, or no-God, whichever the case may be).

If chaplains want to research and read more about humanism, what would you recommend?

Kee: Here are some of my favorite books and authors who shaped my thoughts and beliefs:

- DeGruchy, John W. *Being Human: Confessions of a Christian Humanist.* SCM Press, 2006.
- Estes, Clarissa Pinkola. *Women Who Run with the Wolves.* Ballantine Books, 1992.
- Gilbert, Richard S. *The Prophetic Imperative.* Skinner House Books, 2000.
- Hopkins, Dwight D. *Being Human: Race, Culture, and Religion.* Fortress Press, 2005.

- Irigaray, Luce. ed. *Luce Irigaray Key Writings.* Continuum, 2004.
- Jantzen, Grace M. *Becoming Divine: Toward a Feminist Philosophy of Religion.* Indiana University Press, 1999.
- Welch, Sharon D. *A Feminist Ethic of Risk.* Fortress Press, 2000.
- Wells, Spencer. *The Journey of Man.* Random House, 2002.
- Wright, Conrad. ed., *Three Prophets of Religious Liberalism: Channing, Emerson, Parker.* Beacon Press, 1962.

—Reverend Leslie Kee
Unitarian universalist
Religious humanist
Earth-based spiritualist and activist
Feminist theologian and life-long-learner

CHAPTER 7

Buddhist Spirituality

Buddhists do not recognize or place meaning upon a divine, sacred god. The main goal is to reach spiritual enlightenment through meditation and conscious living. Buddhists do not really believe in a personal god because they accept that nothing remains the same—all is perpetually changing. The Buddhist concept of the divine is not of a specific God but that there is a collective consciousness as a spiritual connectedness to all things. By following the path to enlightenment, the Buddhist develops his or her wisdom, morals, and meditation.[48]

Personal insight replaces belief in a God with the complete study of the laws of cause and effect: *Karma*.[49] Buddhism places great value on an individual's spiritual insight and liberation through critical reflection and various paths and disciplines.[50] In Buddhism, the closest equivalent term to spirituality is the Sanskrit word *bhāvanā*, which means cultivation. This concept of cultivating spirituality does not involve a dualism of spiritual and physical realms. It aims to seek the ultimate truth or nirvana as one frees or empties oneself of all

---

[48] A. G. Holloway, A.G. *Buddhism: The Buddhists Way of Knowing Buddha.* Amazon Kindle e-book, 2014.

[49] Healthcare Chaplaincy, "Handbook of Patient's Spiritual and Cultural Values for Health Care Professionals" (HealthCare Chaplaincy Network. New York, 2013), 22.

[50] Takeuchi Yoshinori, ed., *Buddhist Spirituality: Indian, Southeast Asian, Tibetan, Early Chinese* Volume 8 of *World Spirituality: An Encyclopedic History of the Religious Quest* (New York: Crossroad Publishing, 1997), xiii.

that is profane and cultivates mindful awareness for all that is good and peaceful.[51]

Buddhists believe that our lives are both eternal and exposed to sufferings, impermanence, and uncertainties. They believe a human's life is eternal because each person is reincarnated time and again, and we experience suffering through all our many different lives until full enlightenment is achieved and the rebirth cycle ends. The release from the rebirth cycle can be achieved through Buddhist disciplines and spiritual practices.[52]

Buddha declares, "I teach suffering, its origin, cessation, and path. That's all I teach." The core teachings of Buddha are held in the Four Noble Truths, which he came to realize during a deep meditative state under the Bodhi tree.[53]

1. Dukkha (the truth about suffering)
2. Samudaya (the truth about the source of suffering)
3. Nirodha (the truth about the end of suffering)
4. Magga (the truth about the way to the end of all suffering)

The goal of enlightenment is for the Buddhist to reduce his or her own internal conflict between earthly pleasures and controls that triggers their emotional anxiety, uncontrolled passions, and psychological sufferings. Understanding and acting upon the Four Noble Truths helps them gain this inner control. Once Buddhists are able to mentally and emotionally detach themselves from suffering, it is said that they are beginning to experience nirvana, which is the deep inner joy devoid of fear and negative emotions. Once the individual is fully enlightened, he or she overflows with sympathy for each and every living thing.[54]

Buddhists take refuge in the "three jewels" of Buddha, the dharma, and the saṅgha. The "awakened one" or Buddha refers to historical figures such as Gautama Siddhartha or other Buddhas. But the term

---

[51] Yoshinori, xiii, xiv.
[52] Holloway.
[53] Holloway, chapter 2.
[54] Holloway, chapter 2.

Buddha may also refer to the term for the ultimate goal toward which all beings must strive, transcending the meager physical life while belonging intimately to each individual. The perfection of this spiritual enlightenment is noted to be the universal human vocation.[55]

Dharma or *dhamma* refer to the vision and teachings of the Buddha. The collected sacred scriptures of Buddhism are called sūtras. It is through persistent meditation upon the sūtras that one can discover the deep meaning of the texts and make Buddha's insights their own. This form of personal sanctification is accomplished by overcoming or letting go of the preoccupation with oneself.

The teachings encourage that the accomplishment of the ultimate goal of life is through the practice of *vajrayana* or tantra ("Secret Mantra") meditations.

Mantra is a Sanskrit word stemming from the root word *man*, which means "to think" and the syllable *tra*, which means "tool." Therefore, a mantra can be considered "a tool for thinking." A mantra is a sacred letter form and sound that contains the genetic essence of a specific energy. Buddhist Lama Anagarika Govinda states,

> It is the essence of the creative word, the primal sounds that give shape to the relative reality filling the ultimate reality of the void … The power and effect of a mantra depend on the spiritual attitude, the knowledge and the responsiveness of the individual. The sound of the mantra is not a physical sound (though it may be accompanied by such a one) but a spiritual one. It cannot be heard by the ears, but only by the heart, and it cannot be uttered by the mouth but only by the mind. The mantra has power and meaning only for the initiated … Mantras are not "spells," as even prominent Western scholars repeat again and again … Mantras do not act on account of their own "magic" nature, but only through the mind that experiences them.[56]

---

[55] Yoshinori, xv.
[56] Lama Anagarika Govinda, *Foundations of Tibetan Mysticism* (Boston: Weiser Books, 1969).

In Buddhism, most mantras are pronounced in the original Sanskrit.

There is much importance given to speech (the word/mantra) in all main religions. For example, in the Christian Bible, it reads, "In the beginning was the Word, and the Word was with God, and the Word was God." Similarly, in Hinduism, the sound of *OM* takes as essential part in the creation of the universe. The recitation of mantras is a very important part in tantric practice, as it is used to transform the speech as part of transforming the body, speech, and mind into the respective pure aspects of a Buddha. Like with other tantric practices, they only become really effective after oral transmission from a teacher.[57]

Buddhists purify their minds through tantric meditation practice in order to gain enlightenment, empty their minds, and enjoy the four complete purities of the world, self, enjoyment, and activities. This type of selfless emptiness of worldly attachments allures Buddhists to strive for the tranquility and ultimate truth of nirvāna.

The saṅgha refers to the Buddhist spiritual community that lives by the rules known as the Vinaya and practice Buddhist meditation, seeking wisdom and insight, overcoming human ignorance known as *avidya*, as one transcends the impermanent world.[58] Emotional and physical suffering and the impermanence of our world affect the human condition. The Buddhist desires to overcome these failings by intellectual insights, which lead to kindness, compassion, and inner joy because of the release of the need to selfishly control.

What should a chaplain understand regarding Buddhism's unique spiritual beliefs of reincarnation?

Buddhists believe that, until a soul reaches personal enlightenment, the soul will continue to live, die, and then be reincarnated over and over until enlightenment is achieved. This achievement is accomplished through their own abilities without any divine interaction. Buddhists

---

[57] www.viewonbuddhism.org
[58] Geshe Kelsang Gyatso, *Modern Buddhism: The Path of Compassion and Wisdom, Vol. 2: Tantra* (Glen Spey, NY: Tharpa Publications, 2011), 167–69.

believe in six realms of the universe in which a soul can be reincarnated. Holloway describes these six realms of the universe as:

- *Heaven or the Dwelling of the Gods or "the Devas."* In this realm of pleasure, delightful and long-lived beings reside.
- *The Realm of Humanity.* Even though man suffers, the realm of humanity is deemed as the most privileged state because it is where man can have the highest chance of achieving enlightenment.
- *The Realm of the Titans or Asuras (Angry Gods).* The Titans and Asuras are both aggressive creatures who are always at the mercy of their angry urges.
- *The Realm of the Pretas or the Starving Ghosts.* The pretas are very miserable creatures who are attached to the edges of human existence. They are not able to depart because of their intense attachments. They are not able to fulfill their cravings, which are signified by their big bellies and small mouths.
- *The Realm of Animals.* This is considered an unfavorable realm because man is known to exploit animals—and animals do not possess the required self-awareness to attain enlightenment.
- *The Realm of Hell.* Creatures that stay in this realm are terribly tortured in various imaginative manners, but not forever. A being stays in this realm until he or she has worked off all of his or her bad karma.[59]

Are there unique daily practices in the ways Buddhists express their spirituality?

Daily practices for Buddhist involve meditation or chanting according to the form of Buddhism the Buddhist follows. Allowing for a quiet space and non-disturbed time to observe practices would

---
[59] Holloway, chapter 4.

be appreciated. There is a monthly atonement ceremony on the full moon. Major rituals held at this time include baby blessings, lay and monk ordination, marriage, and death ceremonies.[60]

Do Buddhists have special religious practices or holy days that are recognized?

Special holy days for Buddhists are designated on:

- Buddhist New Year (first full moon day in January, March, or April, depending upon Buddhist sect, celebrated for three days)
- Buddha Day or *Vesak* (first full moon day in May)
- Sangha Day or *Magha Puja Day*, commemorating Buddha's visit to Veruvana Monastery (full moon day in March)
- Dhamma Day or *Asalha Puja Day*, commemorating the "turning of the wheel of the Dharma"—the Buddha's first sermon, which was given at Sarnath Deer Park (full moon day in July)
- Observance Day or *Uposatha* refers to each of the four traditional monthly holy days in Theravada countries (new moon, full moon, and quarter moon days), also known as Poya Day in Sri Lanka.

Buddhists do not have sacraments in the true sense of the term. Buddhism is a religion of enlightenment with the awakening to the true nature of the self being its primary objective. A ritual that may be loosely equated to the ordinance (or sacrament) of Christian baptism is the expression of faith in the three treasures (Buddha, Dharma, and Sangha), which is a symbol of one's becoming a Buddhist.

Buddhists do not outwardly proclaim healing through a faith. However, spiritual peace and liberation from anxiety attained from the awakening to Buddha's wisdom may be an important factor in expediting healing and the recovery process.

---

[60] Healthcare Chaplaincy, 22, 23.

How do Buddhists view or explain Nirvana or the spiritual afterlife?

Jason D. Gray of *The Immortality Project* states,

> There are variations among the Buddhist views of what occurs after death. However, the unifying feature of each is that the cycle of death and rebirth (reincarnation) is to be avoided by achieving nirvana. Nirvana, which means "extinction" or "blowing out," also often translated as "bliss," is the letting go of individual identity and desires.[61] Thus, in the state of nirvana (the state toward which enlightenment drives one) there is no longer an 'individual' and there is no survival of subjective experience …

One striking aspect of the Buddhist view is that there is no soul, as it is understood in the Judeo-Christian or scholastic philosophy traditions. That is, there is no permanent substance or essence which endures after death. Rather the elements of individual identity necessary for Buddhism to have an intelligible view of reincarnation are predicated on, " …an endless array of phenomena making up the individual. These can be divided into five basic categories: physical phenomena, emotions, sensory perceptions, responses to sensory perceptions, and consciousness."[62]

> In the Buddhist view, these elements can continue to exist after the death of the physical body, although they do not take the form of an immortal soul. The phenomena have a finite longevity and are, for instance, dissolved upon the attainment of nirvana or even upon reincarnation (according to one Buddhist tradition).
>
> The biggest difference between Buddhist and Western religious beliefs about the afterlife is not reincarnation. Rather it is the belief that the ideal end state (nirvana) is a

---

[61] John Ashton and Tom Whyte, *The Quest for Paradise*. (San Francisco: HarperCollins, 2001), 46.
[62] Harold Coward, ed., *Life after Death in World Religions*. (Maryknoll, NY: Orbis Books, 1997), 89.

complete dissolution of the self. In the Buddhist picture, the immortality of personal identity and perspective is not desirable. In fact, it is by desiring or clinging to these things that one thwarts the ultimate goal of nirvana.[63]

There are several schools of thoughts about the afterlife within Buddhism. Interested readers are encouraged to read Gray's full article as well as research other scholars on this very interesting topic.

Are there death and dying practices unique to Buddhism that a chaplain should be aware of?

All rituals at death are aimed at promoting human rebirth in the next life as well as preventing lower forms of rebirth taking place. For Buddhists, their state of mind at the time of death is very important, so an environment of calm and peacefulness is desired. If medication while dying affects clarity of the mind, it may not be permitted. Traditionally, there is a three-to-five-day period when the body is not disturbed following death.[64]

---

[63] Jason D. Gray, "Buddhist Views of the Afterlife" The Immortality Project of University of California at Riverside, www.sptimmortalityproject.com.
[64] Healthcare Chaplaincy, 22.

CHAPTER 8

Hindu Spirituality

Hinduism is based upon a wide variety of beliefs and principles that are held together by an attitude of mutual tolerance and belief that all approaches to God are valid.[65] In the Hinduism tradition, achieving Brahman is the spiritual focus. While Hinduism is said to be polytheistic and pantheistic as God is the universe, Brahma is viewed as the "creator" and absolute reality but not a central authority. Hindus believe that Brahma makes all things, but that Brahma also exists immanently in all things as well as transcendently beyond all things.

Brahma is the creator god but is part of a trinity. The god Vishnu, the "preserver" or maintenance god harmonizes between Brahma and the third god, Shiva. Shiva is known as the "destroyer" due to his anger. The earthly incarnate of the Vishnu god is Krishna, who loves cows, plays the flute, and does yoga.

Hinduism's focus is to provide insight into the human condition for successful living by following the law and duty of dharma while seeking salvation and escape from this world. Dharma "governs both the physical and spiritual orders of the universe" while the term *moksha* expresses the concept of deliverance, or salvation, from an unending cycle of rebirth or reincarnation.[66] For Hindus, the goal of

---

[65] Healthcare Chaplaincy, 23.
[66] Gyatso, 167–69.

humankind is to break free of this imperfect work and reunite with God, or Brahman.[67]

Spirituality for Hinduism is most commonly expressed through the study and meditation upon the ancient Sanskrit Vedas or scriptures. For Hindus, the Vedas are ultimate authority. The Vedas do not claim a deity for their inspiration, as the Christian Bible asserts, but were inspired by an eternal sound, *sabda*, which is said to reverberate thought in the universe and gave supernatural revelation for the Vedic passages. The Vedas are comprised of four sections: the Samhitas (a large collection of hymns of praise), the Brahmanas (doctrinal texts for Hindu priests), the Aranyakas (mystical treatises of holy men), and the Upanishads (metaphysical instructions about ultimate Reality).[68]

In an essay on Hindu meditation, Jayaram V writes,

> The purpose of meditation or "dyhana" is to become consciously aware of or investigate into one's own mind and body to know oneself. It is essentially an exclusive, as well as an inclusive process, in which one withdraws one's mind and senses from the distractions of the world and contemplates upon a chosen object or idea with concentration. It is focused thinking with or without the exercise of individual will, in which the mind and the body has to be brought together to function as one harmonious whole. With the help of meditation, we can overcome our mental blocks, negative thinking, debilitating fears, stress and anxiety by knowing their cause and dealing with them. In dyhana we gain insightful awareness whereby we can control over our responses and reactions. Through its regular practice, we come to understand the nature of things, the impermanence of our corporeal existence, the fluctuations of our minds, the source of our own suffering and it possible resolution. The difference between meditation and contemplation is mostly academic. According to, some meditation is an

---

[67] Healthcare Chaplaincy, 23.
[68] Gyatso, 180.

Essential Chaplain Skill Sets

insightful observation and contemplation a concentrated reflection, with detachment being the common factor between the two.

Jayaram V continues,

> Dhyana is a Sanskrit word. "Dhi" means receptacle or the mind and "yana" means moving or going. Dhyana means journey or movement of the mind. If is a mental activity of the mind (dhi). In Hindu philosophy, the mind (manas) is viewed as a receptacle (dhi) into which thoughts pour back and forth from the universal pool of thought forms. According to Hindu tradition, the human mind has the creative potency of God. You become what you think. You are a sum total of your thoughts and desires, not only of this life but also of your past lives. What you think and desire grows upon you, becomes part of your latent impressions (samskaras) and influence the course of your life here and here after. These samskaras determine the future course of your lives as they accompany you to the next world. All your mental actions are part of your karma as much as any physical action. Even the animals have the ability to evolve into higher being through their mental focus.[69]

The basic tenets of Hinduism espouse that, in order to achieve peace and deliverance, a Hindu must follow the dos and don'ts discussed in the sutras and the duties noted in the Vedas.[70] These are:

- Don't lie.
- Don't take advantage of others.
- Don't have indecent or inappropriate attitude toward opposite gender.

---

[69] Jayaram V, "Dhyana or Meditation in Hindu Tradition" www.hinduwebsite.com.
[70] Gokulmuthu Narayanaswamy, *Tenets of Hinduism,* Publisher unknown, 2013. Accessed October 7, 2014. https://scribd.com/doc/223563442/Tenets-of-Hinduism-Gokulmuthu-Narayanaswamy.

- Don't have any unfair possession.
- Don't possess extravagance—lead a simple life.
- Do maintain everything neat and tidy.
- Do maintain discipline and structure to life.
- Do entertain healthy thoughts.
- Do believe in fairness in the world.
- Take care of the environment.
- Take care of animals.
- Take care of people.
- Take care of parents and family.
- Take care of teachers.

If one follows these items, the Hindu is said to be led "to peace and prosperity in individual and social life."

Hindu orthopraxy allows for three differing paths to reach deliverance. One may choose one or more of these: (1) path of knowledge, *jnana marga*, (2) path of action, *karma marga*, and/or (3) path of devotion, *bhakti marga*. All of the paths (knowledge, action, and devotion) are responses and ways to worship Brahma, the Hindu godhead, as every Hindu desires to be fully immersed with Brahma and "strive to appreciate all that they themselves really are and all that everyone else really is in Brahman."[71] As Hindus continually recycle lives, they continue their path toward ultimate deliverance when they final achieve, through their own works, release from this world.

The path of action, karma, is not necessarily the seeking of the life's ultimate purpose (more long term), but karma can also represent simply being attentive and intentional to achieving the current (short-term) purpose in daily activities (e.g., being intentionally focused and not distracted during conversation with others or even while doing mundane daily chores.) Karma is actively seeking meaning and purpose from all activities and goals in life. Hindus view reincarnation as the result of karma (the qualitative value and totality of one's actions and deeds, meritorious or vicious, good or bad). The

---

[71] Saint-Laurent, 170–71.

resultant body in which one is reincarnated reflects the quality of karma one has accrued in the previous life.

Hindu Views of Salvation and Afterlife

Regarding the concept of Hindu afterlife, Jason D. Gray of the Immortality Project at the University of California Riverside writes,

> It is important to keep in mind, when considering the Hindu approaches to the afterlife, that the Hindu religion is polytheistic, lacks a single central text (although the Vedas are universally accepted by Hindus as being divine revelations), and has no specific founder ... Within the Hindu religion there are a diversity of afterlife destinations, and diverse means to reach those destinations ... At the beginning of the first millennium BCE descriptions of the afterlife beliefs of the Hindu faith began to become more detailed. There arose more structure surrounding the rules for ritual knowledge (Veda) and ritual action (Karma) and their role in salvation (i.e. joining the Fathers in Heaven). The Brahmins—the priestly caste in Hindu society—began to take control of these rituals. The path to the World of the Fathers was thought to require not only ritual knowledge and action at the time of death, but in order to be maintained in this realm one's descendants must continue with ritual action. Without the proper action and knowledge one would be reborn again on earth ... Ignorance of the true nature of the self (the essential self) was thought to be the fundamental cause of suffering. In this tradition the essential self is encompassed by three different bodies: the physical body, the subtle body, and the causal body. The physical body: "Like any finite object ... originates in time, grows, changes, declines, and perishes." (Coward, 72) The subtle body, although not permanently associated with the essential self, survives the death of the physical body, records the karma (i.e. all of our deeds) accumulated in past lives, and accounts for reincarnation in the Hindu faith. The subtle body is

> described as being composed of, " ...the five vital forces, the five sense organs, the five organs of action, the mind, and the intellect" (Coward, 73). The third body clothing the essential self is the causal body. The causal body manifests itself in deep sleep. "In this state all individual personality traits and propensities enter into a causal or seed-like condition ... [and they] manifest again in the dream and waking state." (Coward, 73) The separation of the subtle body (which includes the causal body) from the physical body is the definition of death in the Hindu faith. According to the Upanishads, karma was something that is either "worked off" (in the case of bad karma) or "rewarded" (in the case of good karma).

Gray continues,

> The universally accepted elements of the Hindu afterlife tradition seem to be that reincarnation results from selfish and desirous action and that the World of the Fathers is only a temporary state of reward. However, Hinduism is quite different from western religious traditions (cf. the early development of Christianity, which resulted in increased standardization of practices and ideology) in that as it developed it began to accommodate a wider range of approaches to salvation and the afterlife.[72]

Hindu Jayaram V states that there are five steps that determine a Hindu's level of heaven or hell in the afterlife:

Previous Deeds: Bad deeds equal lower worlds and suffering the consequences of evil actions. On the contrary, if good deeds are performed, the deceased will go to the higher sun-filled worlds and enjoy the life there.

---

[72] Gray.

State of Mind at Time of Death: What were the thoughts and desires most predominant in the consciousness of the deceased at time of death? This decides the direction the Jiva will travel and in what form it will attain.

A Jiva that goes to heaven will enjoy the pleasures of heaven. A Jiva or soul that falls into the darker world gets a taste of the horror of the evil it tried to promote on earth, with a multiplier effect and with an intensity and severity that would make it realize the horrors of evil. Thus, in either case, the purpose of heavens and hells is to impart an attitude of wisdom and detachment to the souls.

Jivas can move from heavenly worlds down to the dark worlds and back again. Hindu scriptures are not unanimous about what happens to a soul after it leaves this world. There is uncertainty.

The Time of Death: The time and circumstance of death can achieve higher heavenly realms, (e.g., dying in battle or dying during participation in Hindu rituals or festivals).

The Activities of the Deceased Children: There is Hindu belief that if funeral rites are not fulfilled according to the tradition, the deceased may be delayed on his or her journey to the respective worlds.

The Grace of God: Based upon a Hindu's earthly works, their personal deity may rescue them and place them in a higher or highest heavenly realm in recognition of their meritorious earthly deeds.

Jayaram V explains,

> Death is merely a temporary cessation of physical activity, a necessary means of recycling the resources and energy and an opportunity for the jiva (that part that incarnates) to reenergize itself, review its programs and policies and plan for the next phase of life … According to Hindu scriptures, the solution to the problem of death is not heaven but liberation, and the best way to attain salvation

is through austerities, discipline, devotion, self-surrender and the grace of a guru and God.[73]

According to the Upanishads, Hindus do believe in ghosts and spirits. Bad spirits have the ability to possess bodies and speak through humans. They seek out people of impure minds and unclean habits, generally hanging around deserted buildings, in ancient ruins, and on branches of old trees and graveyards. Good spirits often are waiting to be released from their celestial punishment, loitering near places of religious ceremonies and not harming anyone.

Hindus do believe in evil spells being cast upon others and have tantric exercises to take control of ghosts and spirits in order to drive them away.

Additional Reading on Hindu Afterlife

- Miller, Barbara S. (trans.). *The Bhagavad-Gita*. New York: Bantam Books, 1986.
- Thuruthiyil, Scaria. "Reincarnation in Hinduism."
- www.spiritual-wholeness.org/faqs/reincgen/hindrein.htm

What are some cautions or non-helpful ways chaplains should be aware when ministering to a Hindu?

Chaplains should always strive to provide a supportive and private environment for Hindus to express their spiritual practices. These practices might include reading sacred writings, burning incense, and pictures, prayer beads, or fresh flowers.

It is customary to speak and direct all communication to the primary male spokesman. For chaplains, it is wise to know that Hindus consider prayers for health to be a low form of prayer, while stoicism is preferable. Based upon local customs, specific ceremonies will vary, but forms of prayer, meditating, scripture reading, and recitation are common.[74]

---

[73] Jayaram V.
[74] Healthcare Chaplaincy, 24.

Are there death and dying practices unique to Buddhism that a chaplain should be aware of?

Like Buddhism, Hindus desire a quiet, calm environment as a person is dying. Scriptures from the Gita are often recited to strengthen the person's mind and provide comfort. Religious chanting before and after death is continually offered by family, friends, and priests. Hindus would prefer to die at home or as close to Mother Earth as possible.[75]

Regarding the spiritual assessment of a Hindu, how do Hindus find strength, hope, and resiliency through their spirituality when facing life struggles?

It is often said that Hindus have a holiday for every day of the year, but that would be an understatement! Hindu scholars have listed more than a thousand different Hindu festivals. We will only list the more accepted holy days of Hinduism. Participating in holy days and festivals is especially meaningful to Hindus since they are intended to purify and renew.

Practices during these holy days and festivals may include worship, prayer, processions, magical acts, music, dancing, lovemaking, drinking, eating, and feeding the poor.

- Purnima (day of full moon)
- Janamashtmi or Krishna Jayanti celebrates the birthday of Lord Krishna (in July/August)
- Rama Navami celebrates birthday of Lord Rama (in April)
- Mahashivaratri or Shiva Ratri Festival celebrates the birth of Lord Shiva (on the fourteenth day of the dark half of the lunar month of Phalguna)
- Naurate (nine holy days come twice in a year—April and October)
- Dussehra

---

[75] Healthcare Chaplaincy, 23.

- Diwali Festival of Lights (begins on New Year's Eve and last five days)
- Holi Festival or *Holaka* or *Phagwa* an annual festival commemorating events of Hindu mythology; a time of indulgences and disregard to social norms (in early March)

Some Hindu subsets do believe in faith healings, but others do not. Some also believe that sickness and hardships are God's way of punishing for sins.

There are no sacraments in the Hindu faiths.

CHAPTER 9

Islamic Spirituality

Islam is a monotheistic religion that offers its own distinctive path to God's peace. The Arabic term *Islam* means submission and was designated as the religion's name by Allah during an address to Muslims at Muhammad's farewell. This passage states, "Today I have perfected your system of belief and bestowed My favors upon you in full, and have chosen Islam as the creed for you" (Qur'an 5:3b).

Islam is based upon Five Pillars:

- One pillar of faith
    - confessing and professing that there is no god but God and that Muhammad is the messenger of God
- Four pillars of works
    - performance of ritual prayer
    - payment and the giving of an obligatory charity
    - pilgrimage to Mecca
    - adhering to the annual fast of Ramadan

Muslims believe that Allah established Islam as "the final and complete religion for all of God's human creatures" with the Qur'an as its sole book of scripture. Muslims view the Qur'an as the actual Word of God with the extreme reverence as Christians view Christ himself as the Word of God who entered this world through the Virgin

Mary.[76] The Qur'an informs the Muslims' faith and is integrated into all aspects of their lives. The Qur'an, which means "recitation," is also known to Muslims as *al-Furqān* ("the discernment"), *al-Hudā* (the Guide), the *Umm al-kitāb* (the Mother of Books), or *dhiker Allāh*, (the remembrance of God).[77]

Muslims submit to God in the mosque or *masjid* "the prostration place" and in their homes and workplaces without division between their religion and culture.[78] Islam is enmeshed throughout the Muslim lifestyle. Muslims realize that the true secret for success and life fulfillment is to be totally dependent servants of God.

The Prophet Muhammad serves as the exemplar of Islamic spirituality for all Muslims as he faithfully adhered to the straight path of submission to Allah. The Quran states, "You have indeed a noble paradigm in the Apostle of God for him who fears God and the day of Resurrection, and remembers God frequently" (Qur'an 33:21).

As Islam means "submission," Muslim servitude involves great efforts to remain faithful to the Prophet Muhammad's manner and way of life. Muslims are exhorted, "O you who believe, follow the path shown to you by God, and seek the way of proximity to Him, and struggle in His way: you may have success" (Qur'an 5:34). This struggle, exertion, or sacrifice is but one of the four types of jihads as this form emerges and engages the focus of earnest Muslims throughout their lifetimes.[79] Islam's works-dependent jihad is against materialism and allurements of luxury, with a reward of eternal paradise for those who fought hard and well.

Islam is based on the central doctrine of strict monotheism (*al-tawhīd*) and concerned with God's will (as noted in the Shari'ah, the divine law of Islam). This is displayed outwardly as obedience

---

[76] Seyyed Hossein Nasr, ed., *Islamic Spirituality: Foundations,* Volume 19 of *World Spirituality: An Encyclopedic History of the Religious Quest.* (New York: Crossroad Publishing, 1997), 4.
[77] Nasr, *Foundations*, 6–7.
[78] Saint-Laurent, 135.
[79] Mateen Elass, "Four Jihads" *Christianity Today* (2002). Accessed October 7, 2014. www.haventoday.org/dr-mateen-elass-four-jihads-gd-125.html; also in Saint-Laurent, 138.

Essential Chaplain Skill Sets

to the law, which allows a Muslim to live a balanced and happy life and achieve salvation at the time of death.[80] With Islam, everything becomes spiritual because all actions must be accordance with God's pleasure. One scholar states,

> This conviction creates a world view, a perspective and a unique behavior. It essential means that all actions—from having a shower to picking up litter from the floor—should be referred to the Creator. This establishes a constant awareness, mindfulness and consciousness of God in everything that the Muslim says or does.[81]

The Islamic faith believes that humanity has a spiritual life after physical death, but that salvation is achieved through purification from original sin. In a theological discussion of Islamic beliefs, Rich Wendling and Daniel Shayesteh write that Muslims have an uncertainty about their personal salvation. To support this viewpoint, they write,

> Like the Bible, the Quran teaches that people are descendants of Adam and Eve and are imperfect sinners. However, the Quran also teaches that their god, Allah, inspired sin in humankind (Quran 4:88; 7:16–18; 9:51; 14:4; 16:93; 35:8; 57:22; 74:31; 91:7–9).
>
> Muslims believe that humans are sinners because Allah has willed it … As stated, the Quran teaches that salvation is based on purification by good deeds (Quran 7:6–9). A Muslim can become righteous through prayer, almsgiving, fasting, and living according to the Quran. Yet the Quran also teaches that Allah has predetermined every person's destiny, and one's righteous acts may or may not affect Allah's decision (Quran 57:22). It teaches that everyone, both the righteous and the unrighteous, will

---

[80] Seyyed Hossein Nasr, ed., *Islamic Spirituality: Manifestations*, Volume 20 of *World Spirituality: An Encyclopedic History of the Religious Quest*. (New York: Crossroad Publishing, 1997), xiv.

[81] Tzortis, Hamza Andreas. "What is Islamic Spirituality?" ww.hamzatzortis.com.

be led into hell by Allah, before the righteous will enter heaven (Quran 19:67–72).

Therefore, no Muslim can know his or her eternal destiny in this life. Even Muhammad himself was unsure of his salvation (Quran 31:34; 46:9). Today, whenever Muslims mention the name of Muhammad, they always add the phrase, "Peace be upon him," because Muhammad's eternal destiny is uncertain, and the Muslim must ask Allah to be merciful to him. This contradiction between the Quran's teaching of salvation by works and its teaching of Allah determining salvation, regardless of one's works, results in Islam being the world's most uncertain religion regarding salvation.[82]

The above perspective helps others understand the strict religious disciplines that is noted with followers of Muhammad.

For the Muslim, the intentional and inward spiritual expression of the Muslim's spirit (*rūh*) is very important. The spirit is at the center of man's existence and is the gate leading toward divine transcendence and immanence.[83] The Qur'an states, "So when I have (perfectly) shaped him and blown My spirit (the spirit that I have created) into him, then fall every one of you should bow down to him" (Qur'an 38:72). Unlike the secular understanding of spirituality, Islamic spirituality is the "constant reference to God and ensuring that everything he or she does is in accordance with God's pleasure."[84]

In a discussion of the expression of Islamic spirituality, Seyyed Hossein Nasr writes,

> What can specifically be called Islamic spirituality is the experience and knowledge of this Unity and its realization in thoughts, words, acts, and deeds, through the will, the soul, and the intelligence. This spirituality is ultimately to live and act constantly according to God's Will, to love

---

[82] "Islam's View of Sin and Salvation," www.answersingenesis.org.
[83] Nasr, *Manifestation*, xiii–xiv.
[84] Tzortis.

Him with one's whole being, and finally to know him through that knowledge which integrates and illuminates and whose realization is never divorced from love nor possible without correct action.

The Healthcare Chaplaincy Network states the following about Islam's common beliefs and daily practices.[85]

Islamic Beliefs

- One God, or Allah, is the important principle.
- Complete submission to God.
- Prophet Muhammad and Holy Qur'an.
- A judgment day and life after death.
- Commitment to fast during the holy month of Ramadan: abstaining from food, drink, sexual intercourse, and evil intentions and actions.
- Commitment to attempt a pilgrimage to Mecca (in Saudi Arabia) at least once in lifetime.
- Duty to give generously to poor people.
- Belief in oneness of God.
- Belief in His angels.
- Belief in His books (all the revealed scriptures).
- Belief in His messengers (all of them).
- Belief in hereafter (life after death).
- Belief in the Day of Judgment.
- Belief in reward and punishment.

Islamic Practices

- May engage in prayer five times a day facing Mecca (dawn, midday, midafternoon, sunset, night); face, hands, and feet are washed before prayer.

---

[85] Healthcare Chaplaincy, 16.

- Do not interrupt or walk in front of a Muslim when he/she is saying prayers unless it is an emergency.
- Observance of holy days: Muslims do not work on these holy days. First is the Celebration of the Fast Breaking (*Eid-ul-Fitr*), which is held after the month of fasting (Ramadan or Ramazan) on the first day of the ninth month of the lunar calendar; second holy day is the Celebration of the Sacrifice of Abraham (*Eid-ul-Aha*), which is a three-day celebration beginning on the tenth day of the twelfth month called *Dhul Hijjah*. *Eid-ul-Aha* occurs at the end of the season of pilgrimage to Mecca. These holy days consist of prayer and a short sermon in congregation followed by food, entertainment, feeding of the poor, and visiting the sick and elderly.
- Special days of commemoration: Muslims also observe the death of Prophet Mohammad. The Shiite sect observes the day Iman Ali was assassinated and the Ashora or the martyrdom of Imam Hussein.
- Other days of observance: Muslims also observe the day of Prophet Muhammad's ascension (*Me'rah* and *Asra*); the Night of Power (*Lailat El Ghadr*), and the birthday of Imam Madhi (*Nosfe Sha'ban*).

To Muslims, the many natures and "names" of Allah are important. The Qur'an commands Muslims to call on Allah by his "most beautiful names." Qur'an 7:180 states, "And to Allah belongs the best names, so invoke Him by them. And leave [the company of] those who practice deviation concerning His names. They will be recompensed for what have been doing."

In the Hadith, Muhammad says that there are ninety-nine names of Allah and that anyone who memorizes the list of names will be awarded paradise. "Abu Huraira reported Allah's Messenger as saying: There are ninety-nine names of Allah; he who commits them to memory would get into Paradise. Verily, Allah is Odd (He is one, and it is an odd number) and He loves odd number" (Sahih Muslim 6475).

Essential Chaplain Skill Sets

There are more than ninety-nine names or natures attributed to Allah found in the Qur'an and the Hadith, yet Muhammad never delivered an official list to his followers. Here is a compilation of the ninety-nine names or descriptions of Allah's character and nature with the English meanings to the Arabic transliterations.[86]

1. Ar-Rahman ("The Gracious" or "The Beneficent") Qur'an 1:1; 17:110; 27:30; 59:22
2. Ar-Rahim ("The Merciful") Qur'an 1:1; 2:163; 3:31; 5:98; 12:64; 30:5
3. Al-Malik ("The King" or "The Eternal Lord") Qur'an 20:114; 23:116; 59:23; 114:2
4. Al-Quddus ("The Holy" or "The Most Sacred") Qur'an 59:23; 62:1
5. As-Salam ("The Embodiment of Peace") Qur'an 59:23
6. Al-Mu'min ("The One Who Gives Security" or "The Infuser of Faith") Qur'an 59:23
7. Al-Muhaymin ("The Protector" or "The Preserver of Safety") Qur'an 59:23
8. Al-Aziz ("The Mighty One") Qur'an 3:6; 4:158; 9:40; 59:23: 61:1
9. Al-Jabbar ("The Compeller" or "The Omnipotent One") Qur'an 59:23
10. Al-Mutakabbir ("The Majestic" or "The Dominant One") Qur'an 59:23
11. Al-Khaliq ("The Creator") Qur'an 6:102; 13:16; 39:62; 40:62; 59:24
12. Al-Bari ("The Maker" or "The Evolver") Qur'an 59:24
13. Al-Musawwir ("The Flawless Shaper") Qur'an 59:24
14. Al-Ghaffar ("The Great Forgiver") Qur'an 20:82; 38:66; 39:5; 40:42; 71:10

---

[86] This list is a compilation of the traditionally accepted ninety-nine names of Allah from various references in order to include English transliteration and Qur'an references. References included: "99 names of Allah," www.answeringmuslims.com; http://99namesofallah.name; www.islamcity.org/5855/99-names-of=-allah (accessed May 15, 2017).

15. Al-Qahhar ("The One Who Subdues" or "The All-Prevailing One") Quran 13:16; 14:48; 38:65; 39:4; 40:16
16. Al-Wahhab ("The Supreme Bestower") Qur'an 3:8; 38:35
17. Ar-Razzaq ("The Total Provider") Qur'an 51:58
18. Al-Fattah ("The Opener" or "The Supreme Solver") Qur'an 34:26
19. Al-Alim ("The All-Knowing One") Qur'an 2:158; 3:92; 4:35; 24:41; 33:40; 35:38; 57:6
20. Al-Qabid ("The Withholder" or "The Restricting One") Qur'an 2:245
21. Al-Basit ("The Expander" or "The Extender") Qur'an 2:245
22. Al-Khafid ("The Reducer") Qur'an 56:3
23. Ar-Rafi ("The One Who Exalts" or "The Elevating One") Qur'an 58:11
24. Al-Mu'izz ("The One Who Gives Honor") Qur'an 3:26
25. Al-Mudill ("The One Who Humiliates") Qur'an 3:26
26. As-Sami ("The All-Hearing") Qur'an 2:127; 2:137; 2:256; 8:17; 49:1
27. Al-Basir ("The All-Seeing") Qur'an 4:58; 17:1; 42:11; 42:27; 57:4; 67:19
28. Al-Hakam ("The Impartial Judge") Qur'an 22:69
29. Al-Adl ("The Just" or "The Embodiment of Justice") Qur'an 6:115
30. Al-Latif ("The Gentle One" or "The Knower of Subtleties") Qur'an 6:103; 22:63; 31:16; 33:34; 67:14
31. Al-Khabir ("The All-Aware One") Qur'an 6:18; 17:30; 49:13; 59:18; 63:11
32. Al-Halim ("The Forbearing" or "The Clement One") Qur'an 2:225; 17:44; 22:59; 35:41
33. Al-Azeem ("The Magnificent One" or "The Incomparably Great") Qur'an 2:255; 42:4
34. Al-Ghafur ("The Forgiving") Qur'an 2:173; 8:69; 16:110; 41:32; 60:7
35. As-Shakur ("The Appreciative" or "The Acknowledging One") Qur'an 35:30; 42:23; 64:17
36. Al-Ali ("The Sublime One" or "The Highest") Qur'an 2:255; 4:34; 31:30; 42:4; 42:51

37. Al-Kabir ("The Great One") Qur'an 13:9; 22:62; 31:30; 34:23; 40:12
38. Al-Hafiz ("The Guarding One" or "The Preserver") Qur'an 11:57; 34:21; 42:6
39. Al-Muqit ("The Sustainer") Qur'an 4:85
40. Al-Hasib ("The Reckoning One" or "The One Who Brings Judgment") Qur'an 4:6; 4:86; 33:39
41. Al-Jalil ("The Majestic One" or "The Sublime") Qur'an 55:27
42. Al-Karim ("The Generous" or "The Bountiful One") Qur'an 27:40; 82:6
43. Ar-Raqib ("The Watchful One") Qur'an 4:1; 5:117
44. Al-Mujib ("The Responsive One") Qur'an 11:61
45. Al-Wasi ("The Boundless One" or "The All-Embracing, All-Pervading One") Qur'an 2:115; 2:261; 2:268; 3:73; 5:54
46. Al-Hakim ("The Wise One") Qur'an 2:129; 2: 260; 31:27; 46:2; 57:1; 66:2
47. Al-Wadud ("The Loving One") Qur'an 11:90; 85:14
48. Al-Majid ("The Glorious One") Qur'an 11:73
49. Al-Ba'ith ("The Resurrector" or "The Infuser of New Life") Qur'an 22:7
50. As-Shahid ("The All Observing Witness") Qur'an 4:79; 4:166; 22:17; 41:53; 48:28
51. Al-Haqq ("The Embodiment of Truth") Qur'an 6:62; 22:6; 23:116; 31:30
52. Al-Wakil ("The Advocate" or "The Universal Trustee") Qur'an 3:173; 4:171; 28:28; 33:3; 73:9
53. Al-Qawwi ("The Strong One") Qur'an 22:40; 22:74; 42:19; 57:25; 58:21
54. Al-Matin ("The Firm One") Qur'an 51:58
55. Al-Wali ("The Friend" or "The Protecting Associate") Qur'an 3:68; 4:45; 7:196; 42:28; 45:19
56. Al-Hamid ("The Praiseworthy" or "The Sole-Laudable One") Qur'an 14:1; 14:8; 31:12; 31:26; 41:42
57. Al-Muhsi ("The Reckoner" or "The All-Enumerating One") Qur'an 72:28

58. Al-Mubdi ("The Originator") Qur'an 10:4; 10:34; 27:64; 29:19; 85:13
59. Al-Mu'id ("The Restorer") Qur'an 10:4; 10:34; 27:64; 29:19; 85:13
60. Al-Muhyi ("The Giver of Life") Qur'an 3:156; 7:158; 30:50
61. Al-Mumit ("The Inflictor of Death") Qur'an 7:158; 15:23; 57:2
62. Al-Hayy ("The Eternally Living One") Qur'an 2:255; 3:2; 20:111; 25:58; 40:65
63. Al-Qayyum ("The Self-Subsisting One") Qur'an 2:255
64. Al-Wajid ("The Finder" or "The Pointing One") Qur'an 38:44
65. Al-Majid ("The All-Noble One") Qur'an 85:15
66. Al-Wahid ("The Only One" or "The Unique One") Qur'an 2:163; 5:73; 9:31; 18:110
67. Al-Ahad ("The Indivisible" or "The Sole One") Qur'an 112:1
68. As-Samad ("The Eternal" or "The Supreme Power") Qur'an 112:1
69. Al-Qadir ("The Able" or "The Omnipotent One") Qur'an 6:65; 36:81; 75:40; 86:8
70. Al-Muqtadir ("The All-Authoritative One" or "The Dominant") Qur'an 18:45; 54:42
71. Al-Muqaddim ("The Expediting One") Qur'an 16:61
72. Al-Mu'akhkhir ("The Procrastinator" or "The Delayer") Qur'an 71:4
73. Al-Awwal ("The Very First") Qur'an 57:3
74. Al-Akhir ("The Infinite Last One") Qur'an 57:3
75. Az-Zahir ("The Manifest" Or "The Perceptible") Qur'an 57:3
76. Al-Batin ("The Hidden" or "The Imperceptible") Qur'an 57:3
77. Al-Wali ("The Patron" or "The Governor") Qur'an 13:11
78. Al-Muta'ali ("The Extremely Exalted One") Qur'an 13:9
79. Al-Barr ("The Beneficent" or "The Fountain Head of Truth") Qur'an 52:28
80. At-Tawwab ("The Relenting One") Qur'an 2:37; 2:128; 4:64; 49:12; 110:3
81. Al-Muntaqim ("The Retaliator" or "The Avenger") Qur'an 32:22; 43:41; 44:16
82. Al-Afu ("The Supreme Pardoner") Qur'an 4:99; 4:149; 22:60

83. Ar-Ra'uf ("The Compassionate One" or "The Benign One") Qur'an 3:30; 9:117; 57:9
84. Malik-ul-Mulk ("The Possessor of Sovereignty" or "The Owner") Qur'an 3:26
85. Dhul-Jalali-wal-ikram ("The Possessor or Lord of Majesty") Qur'an 55:27; 55:78
86. Al-Muqsit ("The Just One" or "The Equitable") Qur'an 3:18; 7:29
87. Al-Jami ("The Gatherer") Qur'an 3:9
88. Al-Ghani ("The Self-Sufficient One") Qur'an 2:263; 3:97; 39:7; 47:38; 57:24
89. Al-Mughni ("The Enricher") Qur'an 9:28
90. Al-Mani ("The Preventer" or "The Defender") Qur'an 67:21
91. Ad-Darr ("The Afflicter" or "The Distressor") Qur'an 6:17
92. An-Nafi ("The Benefactor" or "The Propitious") Qur'an 30:37
93. An-Nur ("The Prime Light" or "The One Who Guides") Qur'an 24:35
94. Al-Hadi ("The Guide") Qur'an 22:54; 25:31
95. Al-Badi ("The Incomparable One" Or "The Unique One") Qur'an 2:117; 6:101
96. Al-Baqi ("The Everlasting One") Qur'an 55:27
97. Al-Warith ("The Eternal Inheritor") Qur'an 15:23
98. Ar-Rashid ("The Guide to the Right Path") Qur'an 2:256
99. As-Sabur ("The Patient One" or "The Extensively Enduring One") Qur'an 2:153

Another way that Islam expresses its spirituality is through repetition of common prayers with a focus of praying the *Salat* prayer five times a day.[87] These are referred to as

- Salat al-Fajr, the morning or dawn prayer, which is said after dawn and before sunrise.

---

[87] The prayers of Salat as well as the common supplications or prayers of Islam (in original Arabic and English transliterations) are easily available as electronic sources through a simple Internet search.

- Salat al-Zuhr, the noon or early afternoon prayer, which is said when the sun begins to decline.
- Salat al-Asr, the mid-afternoon prayer.
- Salat al-Maghrib, the sunset prayer, which is said immediately after the sun sets.
- Salat al-Isha, the night prayer said between the red glow after sunset and extends to midnight or before going to bed.

Before times of prayer, Muslims will appropriately wash their hands and exposed body areas as needed in a process called *wudzu*, or ablution. Common prayerful invocations and supplications (dua's) to Allah are said throughout the day as well as during Friday service times. These supplications are considered very worshipful and might include the following:[88]

> Allah is the greatest ("Allah-hu-Akbar")
> O Allah, glorified, praiseworthy. And blessed is your name and high is your majesty and no deity worthy of worship except you. I seek Allah's protection from the rejected Satan.
> In the name of Allah, the most Kind and the most Merciful. Praise is only for Allah, Lord of the Universe. The most Kind, the most Merciful. The master of the Day of Judgement. You alone we worship and to you alone we pray for help. Show us the straight way, the way of those whom you have blessed. Who have not deserved your anger, nor gone astray. (Surah 1, Al-Fatiha)
>
> He is Allah, the only one. Allah helps and does not need help. He did not produce a child, and He was not born of anyone. There is no one equal to Him. (Surah 112, Al-Iklaas)

---

[88] Saying the daily prayers (*salaah* or *salat*) in the Islamic tradition is unique. References for the traditional Islamic prayer in English transliteration included: "Salaah English transliteration and translation (Namaaz prayer) www.milligazette.com; "How to perform Salaah (Prayer) www.icorlando.org/pdfs/How_to_perform_Salaah.pdf; and "What to say in Salaah (Prayer)," http://www.islamcan.com/salat/duas/index.shtml (accessed May 15, 2017).

Allah is the greatest ("Allah-hu-Akbar")

Glory to my Lord the Exalted.

Allah listens to him who praises Him. Oh our Lord, all praise is to you.

Allah is the greatest ("Allah-hu-Akbar")

Oh Allah, glory be to you, the most High.

Oh Allah, forgive me and have mercy on me [repeat at least three times]

Allah is the greatest ("Allah-hu-Akbar")

Glory to my Lord, the most high [repeat three times]

All compliments, all physical prayer, and all worship are for Allah. Peace

be upon you, Oh Prophet, and Allah's mercy and blessings be upon you. Peace be on us and on all righteous slaves of Allah. I bear witness that no one is worthy of worship except Allah and I bear witness that Muhammad is His slave and Messenger [Tashahhud].

Allah is the greatest. Allah is the greatest.

Oh Allah, exalt Muhammad and on the family and true followers of Muhammad as you did exalt Abraham and his family and his followers. Surely, you are the praiseworthy, the Great. O Allah, bless Muhammad and his followers as you blessed Abraham and his followers. You are Most Praiseworthy, the Exalted. [Darood]

Oh Lord, make me and my children keep up prayers, Our Lord, accept our prayer,

Our Lord, forgive me and my parents and all the Believers on the Day of Judgement.

Peace and mercy of Allah be on you.

It is common that while these invocations are recited by memory, the prayer sits, kneels, stands, and lies prostrate. Various chapters from the Qur'an are also often read between prayer sections.

What are some cautions or non-helpful ways chaplains should be aware when ministering to a Muslim?

Chaplains are encouraged to explore what practices are most important to Muslim individuals. Be aware that some customs prohibit handshakes or any contact between opposite genders.

Friday is considered the holiest day for Muslims, and a congregational prayer (Jum'a Prayer) takes place at noon. Since a highly important way for Muslims to express their spirituality is through multiple daily prayers, providing a quiet environment for them to do so would be greatly appreciated. Having a *qibla* sign pointing to Mecca (east) is also suggested.

Are there death and dying practices unique to Islam that a chaplain should be aware of?

Muslims believe that death is controlled by Allah. The confession of sins and begging for forgiveness often occurs in the presence of family upon death. As the moment of death nears, recitation of the Islamic creed is generally performed. To the devout Muslim, it is very important to appropriately wash the deceased. The washing (Ghosl El May'yet) is performed by a Muslim of the same gender (men wash deceased males, and women wash deceased females). After death and washing of the body, the body is wrapped in a clean white cloth. The cloth fabric is often muslin.

What are some additional references for chaplains to use to learn more about Islam, ministering to Muslims, and Islamic chaplaincy?

If you are not of the Muslim faith, having resources available to you, such as contact information to your local mosque and imam is wise. Additional resources can also be obtained at the Association of Muslim Chaplains (associationofmuslimchaplains.com) and Islamic Society of North America (www.isna.net).

There is also a text available specifically on Muslim chaplaincy: Gilliat-Ray, Sophie. *Understanding Muslim Chaplaincy.* New York: Routledge, 2013.

CHAPTER 10

Jewish Spirituality

The Jewish faith is monotheistic. All of Judaism believes in one, all-powerful God who created the universe and communicated the commandments to the prophet Moses on Mount Sinai. These writings comprise the Torah. For Jews, these commands have priority to be obeyed and fulfilled above all other personal rights and individual pleasures.[89]

The Jewish faith tradition pursues God's shalom or peace. In the Torah, which serves as the charter for Judaism, the psalmist writes, "Depart from evil and do good; seek peace and pursue it" (Psalm 34:14 NASB). Judaism does not specifically account for a set of beliefs in which a Jew may find and achieve eternal salvation.[90] However, Jews do seek a covenant relationship with a transcendent, providential, and interactive Lord. Following the *mitzvah* or commandments of the law as laid forth in the Torah, the godly principles for living and social harmony give Jews a guide for the external and internal connectedness with others and the divine God, Yahweh. The Jewish faith is monotheistic in theology and genealogy from Abraham of the Torah.

Judaism does believe in a spiritual life after physical death, but

---

[89] Healthcare Chaplaincy, 19.
[90] M. R. Wilson, "Judaism" in *Evangelical Dictionary of Theology* 2nd ed., ed. Walter A. Elwell (Grand Rapids: Baker Academic, 2001).

traditional Judaism does not maintain that humanity is doomed by original sin and that humanity does not need personal salvation by a Messiah. The Torah reads, "If you do good, won't there be special privilege? And if you do not do good, sin waits at the door. It lusts after you, but you can dominate it" (Genesis 4:7).

In Judaism, to rule over sinful behaviors and choices is accomplished by man's free will choice of doing good deeds. One Jewish writer's theological viewpoint on this topic is, "No matter what a person does he will get Heaven only if G-d had previously chosen him to get Heaven! Everyone else goes to eternal hell! In Judaism, it is entirely up to you. If you do good, you will get good."[91]

Part of Jewish spirituality is the outward expression of their faith. Jews possess several distinct verbal, symbolic, and nonverbal methods to express their faith and spirituality. One method is through the faith symbols that are traditionally worn or by the application of the *mezuzah*. A *mezuzah* is a small scroll receptacle that is placed on doorposts and mantels as an outward expression informing others of the faith represented in the home or business.

Another method of spirituality expression and development is the Jewish observance of the Sabbath or *Shabbat*. In following the example, as noted in the biblical record of Genesis, Jews rest one day a week as God rested after His creation was complete. The Jewish observance of Shabbat is very spiritual as they intentionally make time to meditate, pray, and seek God's peace from sundown on Friday to sundown on Saturday each week. This provides an inner "opportunity for regaining balanced perspectives, restoring proper priorities, and becoming more fully themselves, renewed and refreshed."[92]

Jews also outwardly express their deep respect and reverence for God in the way they write God's name. In writings, Jews use the descriptor *G-d* when referring to their Yahweh Lord. This comes from interpretation of Deuteronomy 12:3–4, which states that the

---

[91] www.beingjewish.com.
[92] Saint-Laurent, 78.

Israelites should write out God's name where it might be discarded or erased. This traditionally meant God's Hebrew name *Yahweh*, but the English translation is also abbreviated.

Another very important traditional practice is the participation in the annual Seder meal held at Passover. Symbolism of the Jewish faith abounds in the elements of the meal. Traditionally, there are multiple elements of the Seder meal that symbolize and reflect the exodus of the Hebrew people (later known as Israelites and Jews) from captivity in Egypt. Once settled at the table for the Seder meal, and following the recitation of *kiddush* as a benediction, a person is selected to recount the story of Abraham, Isaac, and Jacob and the resultant suffering and persecution in Egypt.

During the meal, four cups of wine are served at different times. These cups are the spiritual expression of the Israelites deliverance and freedom (Exodus 6:6–7). These symbolize four great merits that occurred while the Israelites were in exile: (1) They did not change their Hebrew names; (2) they continued to speak their own language, Hebrew; (3) they remained highly moral; (4) and they remained loyal to one another. Wine is used because it is a symbol of joy and happiness.

The Seder meal itself is comprised of various foods with different historical meanings. First is the appetizer, or *Karpas*, which might be a small portion of onion, a boiled potato, or even parley, lettuce, or watercress. The *Karpas* is dipped in salt water and eaten. The salt water symbolizes the suffering and tears of the Hebrew ancestors, while the *Karpas* represents hope that is found in springtime, redemption, and the renewal of life.

The breaking of Matzah bread is done next. One of three whole pieces of Matzah is broken. It is broken into two unequal pieces with the larger portion set aside for later use. This breaking symbolizes G-d's splitting of the Red Sea during the Hebrew exodus several days after leaving Egypt. As the Matzah is broken, this symbolizes humility. It will be eaten as "bread of poverty."

Next is the telling of the story of the Exodus from Egypt, which is called the *Haggadah*. This would include a brief review of history, a description of the Israelites' suffering, the plagues that came upon the Egyptians, and a list of the miracles performed by the Almighty for the redemption of His chosen people. After a ritual washing of hands (*Rochtzah*) and drinking a second cup of wine, the Matzah is partaken while reciting the special blessing "al achilat matzah."

Bitter herbs, usually horseradish or bitter lettuce, symbolize the bitterness of the Egyptian bondage. The herbs are dipped in *charoset*. *Charoset* is commonly made from a mixture of chopped apples, nuts, cinnamon, and wine, which symbolize the building mortar the Israelites used in captivity. This is followed by the eating of a small bitter herb, often Romaine lettuce, in a matzah sandwich.

Afterwards, the holiday meal (*Shulchan Orech*) is served, which traditionally begins with a roasted or hard-boiled egg (*Beitzah*) dipped into salt water to symbolize the cycle of life and the hope of new beginnings. After the egg is eaten, an entrée of roasted lamb shank or a roasted beet entrée is served. The meat or redness of the beet resembles the blood sacrifices of atonement, which the Israelites offered to Yahweh per the religious practices mentioned in the Talmud.

The larger portion of the broken matzah is now taken and eaten as a dessert (*afikoman*). This symbolizes the Paschal lamb. After this is eaten, no other food or drink is consumed except for the two remaining cups of wine. While the third cup of wine is filled, a special blessing of grace is offered. As the third cup is consumed, special recitations and songs of praise are given. After reciting the Hallel, the fourth cup of wine is taken. At the conclusion of the Seder meal ceremony, all then say *"Leshanah haba'ah bee-rushalayim"* which means "next year in Jerusalem."

The majority of Jews are unaffiliated to Orthodox, Conservative, or Reform Judaism, but they see Judaism as their general identity. While Orthodox Jews strictly adhere to the written and oral laws, Conservative Jews see revelation as divinely inspired but desire Judaism to change to fit with more modern times.

Prayers for the sick can be an important part of faith expression during illness. The most common prayer used in this context is called *micheberach or Mi Sheberakh*. One translation from Hebrew is

> May the One who blessed our ancestors; Patriarchs Abraham, Isaac, and Jacob, Matriarchs Sarah, Rebecca, Rachel, and Leah—bless and heal the one who is ill: _____. May the Blessed One overflow with compassion upon him/her.

The Shema is another commonly recited prayer or statement of faith and allegiance to One God. It is normally said in three parts (paragraphs) and stems from the Talmud passages of Deuteronomy 6:4–9 and 11:13–21.[93] The first part speaks to "an expanded level of consciousness, where Godliness is visibly present. The second paragraph speaks to a lower state of mind, where Godly revelation is absent."[94]

The Shema, Paragraph 1

> Hear, Israel! The Lord is our G-d, the Lord is One! (Blessed is the Name of His glorious kingdom for ever and ever.) You shall love Adonai your G-d with all your heart and with all your soul and with all your might. And these words that I command you today be in your heart. You shall teach them diligently to your children, and you shall speak of them when you are sitting at home, and when you walk along the way, and when you lie down and when you rise up. You shall bind them as a sign on your hand, and they shall be for frontlets (jewels) between your eyes. You shall write them on the doorposts of your house and on your gate. (Deuteronomy 6:4–9)

---

[93] For more information of the Shema's proclamation of Jewish faith and its blessings: https://shofar.org.com; and www.jewishvirtuallibrary.org/the-shema.
[94] Chaim Miller, *Torah: The Five Books of Moses with Complete Haftarah Cycle* (Brooklyn: Lifestyle Books, 2011), 1131.

The Shema, Paragraph 2

(This part repeats themes from Part 1 but adds promises or rewards and punishments):

> And it shall come to pass if your surely listen to the commandments that I command you today, to love the Lord your G-d and to serve him with all your heart and all your soul,
> That I will give rain to your land, the early and the late rains, that you may gather in your grain, your wine and your oil.
> And I will give grass in your fields for your cattle and you will eat and you will be satisfied.
> Beware, lest your heart be deceived and you turn and serve other gods and worship them.
> And anger of the Lord will blaze against you, and he will close the heavens and there will not be rain, and the earth will not give you its fullness, and you will perish quickly from the good land that the Lord gives you.
> So you shall put these, my words, on your heart and on your soul; and you shall bind them for sings on your hands, and they shall be for frontlets between your eyes. You shall teach them to your children, and you shall speak of them when you sit at home, and when you walk along the way, and when you lie down and when you rise up. You shall write them on the doorposts of your house and on your gates. In order to prolong your days and the days of your children on the land that the Lord promised your fathers that he would give them, as long as the days that the heavens are over the earth. (Deuteronomy 11:13–21)

The Shema, Paragraph 3

This third part speaks of the fringes (Tzitzit) on their garments, which are to remind them of the commandments as well as to fulfill the mitzvah.

> And the Lord spoke to Moses, saying, Speak to the children of Israel and say to them,
>
> They should make themselves tzitzits (tassels) on the corners of their clothing throughout their generations, and give the tzitzit of each corner a thread of blue. And they shall be tzitzit for you, and when you look at them you will remember all the Lord's commandments and do them and not follow after your heart and after your eyes which lead you astray.
>
> In order to remember and do all my commandments, and be holy for your G-d. I am the Lord, your G-d, who led you from the land of Egypt to be a G-d to you; I am the Lord, your God. (Numbers 15:37–41)

Besides special prayers and customs like the Seder meal, Jews also celebrate holy days:

- Rosh Hashanah (Jewish New Year)
- Yom Kippur (Day of Atonement)—no eating or drinking.
- Sukkot (weeklong Festival of Tabernacles)
- Chanukah (eight-day Festival of Lights)
- Purim (commemorates the Fast of Queen Ester)
- Pesach/Passover (weeklong Holiday of Freedom)
- Shavuot/Pentecost (Holiday of Revelation)
- Fast Days of Mourning: Asara B'tevet, Tzom Gedalia, Shiva Asar BTamuz, and Tisha B'Av.

Orthodox Jews believe that the Torah is divine and unalterable. They believe in a strict and traditional interpretation of the Torah and the laws and commandments. Corporate worship and prayers in synagogues and temples are especially meaningful.

CHAPTER 11

Christian Spirituality

The monotheistic Christian faith originates from the followers of Jesus Christ, the prophesied Messiah for God's chosen Hebrew people, the Israelites. The existence of Jesus of Nazareth is well documented in secular historical records. The writings of first century Roman historian Flavius Josephus being just one.[95] Even atheist historians, such as Gerd Lüdemann, who dispute the divine resurrection of Jesus, have concluded that Jesus of Nazareth did in fact exist as a historical figure.

Central to Christianity is the belief that the death, burial, and divine resurrection of Jesus Christ allow for the eternal salvation of humanity. Christianity is founded upon God's agape love for mankind and the sacrifice of Christ. The Messiah not only came to abolish the works-oriented Hebrew-Jewish sacrificial system, but the Messiah came to be the faith-based Savior for all of humankind, Jews, and Gentiles (non-Jews).

The Core Beliefs of the Christian Faith

At the core of Christianity are beliefs that stem from the canonized Holy Bible. The following is a composite of many doctrinal statements

---

[95] Flavius Josephus, *The Complete Works of Flavuis Josephus*, 2014, e-book.

of Christian churches and Christian organizations with supportive biblical references:

- Christians believe the Bible, in the Old and New Testament scriptures, to be inspired, the only infallible, true, and authoritative Word of God (John 1:1; 2 Timothy 3:16).
- Christians believe that there is only one holy God, who is eternally existent in three persons: Father, Son, and Holy Spirit. Christians believe in God the Father, the Almighty, maker of heaven and earth, of all that is, seen and unseen (Deuteronomy 6:4; Isaiah 44:8; 45:18; Mark 12:29; James 2:19).
- Christians believe in the deity of our Lord Jesus Christ, the only Son of God. For Christians and their salvation, Christ came down from heaven, was incarnate of the Holy Spirit and the Virgin Mary, and became truly human (Matthew 1:18–25; Luke 2:1–20). Being fully God and perfect man, He performed miracles and lived a sinless life.
- Christians believe Jesus Christ suffered a vicarious and atoning death through the shedding of His blood. He was buried and on the third day was resurrected in His body; after which, He ascended to be seated at the right hand of the Father (Mathew 27:32–56; Luke 22; Acts 1:9–11). He will come again in glory to judge the living and the dead, and his kingdom will have no end.
- Christians believe that mankind was originally created in the image and likeness of God, and free from sin (Genesis 1:26). Through the temptation of Satan, they transgressed the command of God and fell from their original righteousness, whereby all people have inherited a sinful nature that is opposed to God and are thus under condemnation (Genesis 3). As soon as they are capable of moral action, they become actual transgressors.
- Christians believe that for the salvation of lost and sinful people, the regeneration of that person by the Holy Spirit indwelling is absolutely essential (Ezekiel 36:27; Isaiah 63:11;

John 16:13; Romans 8:9, 11; 1 Corinthians 3:16; Ephesians 5:18; Galatians 4:6, 5:18, 22; 2 Timothy 1:14).
- Christians believe in the present ministry of the Holy Spirit that indwells within the Christian. This indwelling and personal connection with God enables the believer to live a more Christlike and pleasing life through the help of the Holy Spirit.
- Christians believe that the Holy Spirit is fully God and is worshipped and glorified with the Father and Son. Christians believe that the Holy Spirit divinely inspired the scriptures, convicts the world of sin, righteousness, and judgment, and leads Christ's universal Church of believers in truth (2 Timothy 3:16–17). Christians believe that the Holy Spirit is the Teacher and Comforter sent by Jesus Christ.
- Christians believe that salvation comes through Jesus Christ alone. Christians believe that salvation involves the redemption of the whole person and is offered freely to all who exercise faith in Jesus Christ (John 3:16). Christians believe in the eternal resurrection of both the saved and those who do not believe (unsaved), but those who are saved (believe in Christ's gospel message) will remain through eternity in the presence of God while those who are not saved will live eternally in the absence of God (damnation).
- Christians believe in the spiritual unity of believers in the Lord Jesus Christ as one holy catholic (universal) and apostolic church, Christ's Body and Bride ministering reconciliation to a lost world (Romans 12:16, 14:19; Acts 4:32; Ephesians 4:3; Philippians 2:2). As ambassadors for the kingdom of God and the church, Christians affirm that evangelism and engagement in societal issues are both part of the Christian duty; both are necessary expressions of their doctrines of God and humanity, their love for their neighbors and their obedience to Jesus Christ and his teachings (John 14:10; 2 Corinthians 5:20; Philippians 2:4; 1 Peter 3:15).

To recap and clarify the above tenets of Christianity: Christianity is a monotheistic religion believing in the one and only Creator God. Christianity is also prominently grounded upon the biblical gospel message of Jesus Christ as being a divine part of the only holy, divine, and triune God. This divine "three-in-one" trinity is comprised of God the Father, God the Son, and God the Spirit.[96] Christian theology states that Jesus Christ voluntarily gave up part of this divine nature to be born in human form through a virgin birth and then lived and sacrificially died for all of humanity's sin.[97]

Jesus Christ resurrected after his crucifixion and death and returned to full deity with God.[98] This act of the messianic Christ fulfilled many of the prophecies and sacrificial commands as recorded throughout the Hebrew Bible (Jewish Tanakh), which is also known as the Holy Bible's Old Testament Scriptures.

For the Christian faith, the God-inspired and inerrant Holy Bible states that all of humanity is separated from God and needs reconciliation by a Savior. This perspective of human depravity is plainly stated by the Apostle Paul: "For all have sinned and fall short of the glory of God" (Romans 3:23 NKJV). Paul also states that eternal atonement is freely available for all who believe in Christ and the message of the Gospel. Toward this point, he writes, "For the wages of sin is death, but the free gift of God is eternal life in Christ Jesus our Lord" (Romans 6:23 NKJV).

The above Christian premise is based upon a triune nature of God and God's grace, agape love, and boundless mercy. It is recorded, "For God so loved the world, that He gave his only begotten Son, that whoever believes in Him shall not perish, but have eternal life" (John 3:16 NKJV). Based on these teachings, the Christian salvation is faith-based, Christ-centered, and independent of religious works as other faith traditions subscribe. The biblical understanding of

---

[96] Wayne Grudem, *Systematic Theology: An Introduction to Biblical Doctrine* (Grand Rapids: Zondervan, 1994), 226–61.
[97] Grudem, 529–607.
[98] Millard J. Erickson, *Christian Theology,* 2nd ed. (Grand Rapids: Baker Academic, 1998), 677–841.

Christianity is fully exclusive upon the belief of the actions of Jesus Christ. Christian salvation is not pluralistic or inclusive of other spiritual paths for eternal salvation but solely through the merits of Jesus Christ.

Eternal salvation occurs for Christians when all people:

1. Personally understand they were born with a sinful and selfish nature, which separates them from experiencing a personal, interactive relationship with God and each soul is in desperate need of atonement.
2. Personally and exclusively ask Christ who is the human-divine mediator to forgive them and graciously grant them salvation. As individuals acknowledge their need for personal atonement and simply pray for God to help and spiritually restore them into righteousness before Him, they become Christians (i.e., "like Christ").

ABC is a common acronym for the Christian path toward redemption and eternal salvation.

- *Admit.* Acknowledge one's own sin and inability to work one's way into God's grace and holy presence (Romans 3:10–18, 3:23).
- *Believe.* Believe that Christ's death, burial, and resurrection is God's gift for man's forgiveness from sin (John 3:16).
- *Confess.* Confess one's faith in Jesus Christ as Savior and Lord to others (Romans 10:9–10).

Here is a simple prayer that many Christians use to personally and intentionally ask for God's salvation:

> Father, I know that I have broken your laws and my sins have separated me from you. I am truly sorry, and now I want to turn away from my past sinful life toward you. Please forgive me, and help me avoid sinning again. I believe that your son, Jesus Christ died for my sins, was

resurrected from the dead, is alive, and hears my prayer. I invite Jesus to become the Lord of my life, to rule and reign in my heart from this day forward. Please send your Holy Spirit to help me obey you, and to do your will for the rest of my life. In Jesus's name I pray, Amen.

Christian spirituality is expressed in many forms. Following the teachings of Jesus Christ is of paramount importance to the expression of Christianity, as well as observance of the two ordinances of the faith: Communion (Lord's Supper) and baptism. Reverent worship in church settings, prayer, meditation upon biblical passages for life direction, as well as listening and responding to the Holy Spirit's promptings and guidance in life are core to enhancing and expressing Christian spirituality. For many Christian believers, practicing spiritual disciplines (prayer, worship services, reading Holy Scripture) help connect them to the transcendent yet personal God.

For Christians, personal interaction with their Creator and Savior is paramount. While eternal salvation through Christ's actions results in a believer's justification before a Holy God, the steady and continuous discipline of humble learning about Christ helps the believer live a more Christlike and sanctified life on earth. This is a life of progressive sanctification. One Christian ministry describes this life as following six critical areas: humility, honesty, repentance, forgiveness, obedience, and seeking His kingdom first in our daily decisions.[99]

Humility. The Scriptures explain that God opposes the proud but gives grace to the humble (James 4:6). In humility, therefore, we seek His grace by admitting our own great need, throwing off our self-sufficiency and bowing prayerfully before our Lord.

Honesty. Confession of sin avails us of God's forgiveness and cleansing (1 John 1:9). Experiencing personal revival always involves honestly dealing with our sins, both those committed against God and those committed against other people.

---

[99] www.LifeAction.org.

Repentance. Seeking God's face is not merely an exercise in rituals or words; it is really a change of direction. Repentance involves turning from our sins so we can obey God instead of self. As Paul wrote to the Ephesians, we must "put off" the old self and "put on the new identity Christ died to provide for us (Ephesians 4:17–24).

Forgiveness. Experiencing God's forgiveness is one of the greatest blessings of the Christian life, and God requires that we pass that from us (Ephesians 4:32). As we come close to God for spiritual renewal, we must release the bitterness we hold, clear our sin accounts with others, extend forgiveness to those who have wronged us, and seek it from those we have wronged.

Obedience. From a position of humble repentance, we are now ready to say yes to Christ in every category of our lives. He is worthy of our obedience in everything—from daily habits to major decisions. Even our thoughts and motivations are important to Him (Luke 6:46).

Seeking His Kingdom First. Obedience to God leads us to a complete reprioritization of life. The ultimate aim of spiritual renewal is that each of us would walk with God, demonstrate His love in a dark world, and be a part of fulfilling the Great Commission task in our generation (Matthew 6:33; Mark 16:15).[100]

For followers of Christ, the above disciplines allow them to strive toward faithfully living and expressing their spirituality in all aspects of their lives. This is achieved because their worldview perspective changes to a Christian worldview that sees all of life through the eyes of their Creator Lord.

---

[100] www.LifeAction.org *Ignite* newsletter (Spring 2016).

What are some cautions or non-helpful ways that chaplains should be aware of when ministering to a Christian?

Professionally, chaplains are trained to work with individuals of all faiths and spiritual beliefs. However, Christians—especially evangelical and more charismatic Christians (e.g., denominations such as Baptist, Pentecostal, and Assembly of God)—may not be as accepting of chaplains who are not professed Christians. This may not negate wonderful ministry of deep soul care, but the practice of meaningful prayer is critical. Prayer is highly important to Christians when they are ill and struggling with issues of life. If the ministering chaplain is not truly able to believe in and pray to the Christian's God (Yahweh), then it would be recommended that chaplains ask how they may seek other pastoral support and resources for their spiritual needs.

Regarding the spiritual assessment of a Christian, how does the Christian find strength, hope, and resiliency through their spirituality when facing life struggles?

Sacraments: Christians find great strength and comfort through participation in the sacraments. Chaplains should spend time to fully understand the Christian and Catholic sacraments. Evangelicals and Protestants adhere to two sacraments: the Lord's Supper (Communion) and Baptism. The Catholic faith tradition recognizes seven sacraments: baptism, confirmation, Holy Eucharist (Communion), penance, matrimony, holy orders, and anointing of the sick.

Holy Days

Participation in holy days is also a way Christians express their spirituality. For Christians, there are two primary holy days:

- Christmas (December 25)—the celebration of Jesus's birth in human form
- Easter Sunday—the celebration of Jesus's death for humanity's sins, burial, and resurrection back to God the Father's heavenly presence.

For Catholics, holy days are:

- Sundays
- Feast of Mary the Mother of God (January 1)
- Easter Sunday
- Ascension Thursday (forty days after Easter Sunday)
- Assumption of Mary into heaven (August 15)
- All Saints' Day (November 1)
- Feast of the Immaculate Conception (December 8)
- Christmas, birth of Christ (December 25)

What are some common methods that Christian patients utilize to help them cope as well as discover deeper purpose, meaning, and satisfaction in life?

A core element in what makes Christians resilient and hopeful in times of struggle and grief is understanding the character and nature of God. This is also evident within the religion of Islam with the ninety-nine names of Allah (discussed in chapter 9). For Christians, salvation stems from what God graciously does for them instead of what believers have to do or achieve for salvation (as noted in other belief systems). This divine agape love, grace, and mercy shown by God—as well as the personal relationship through Christ—makes the Christian eternally grateful and humble with the ability to truly and unselfishly love others. This all occurs due to God's love and power being bestowed to the Christian by God and not vice versa.

Based upon the specific character of God, various alternate names have been given to Him, which are very meaningful to Christ's followers:

- Adonai (Lord) Genesis 15:2; Judges 6:15
- El or Elohim (God is Creator, Mighty, Strong, Prominent) Genesis 17:7; 31:29; Numbers 23, 19; Deuteronomy 5:9; Jeremiah 31:33; Nehemiah 9:17; Psalm 139:19
- El Elyon (Most High) Deuteronomy 26:19
- El Gibhor (The Messiah Who is Mighty) Isaiah 9:6; Revelation 19:15
- El Olam (Everlasting God) Psalm 90:1–3
- El Roi (God Who Lives and Sees All) Genesis 16:13
- El Shaddai (God Almighty) Genesis 49:24; Psalm 132:2,5
- YHWH, Yahweh, Jehovah (Lord) (The Lord is, above all, ever-present and near.) Exodus 3:14; Deuteronomy 6:4; Psalm 25:11, 31:3; 107:13; Daniel 9:14
- Yahweh or Jehovah Jireh (My Provider) Exodus 15:26
- Yahweh or Jehovah M'Kaddesh (My Sanctifier) God cleanses and makes us holy before Him; Ezekiel 37:28
- Yahweh or Jehovah Nissi (My Banner) commemorates the Israelites desert victory over the Amalekites; Exodus 17:15
- Yahweh or Jehovah Rapha (My Healer) Exodus 15:26
- Yahweh or Jehovah Rohi (My Shepherd) Psalm 23:1
- Yahweh or Jehovah Shalom (My Peace Giver) names given by Gideon to the altar; Judges 6:24; Christ is also known as the Prince of Peace since true salvation brings deep inner peace
- Yahweh or Jehovah Shamma (My Friend; The Lord is There) Ezekiel 4:1–4; 48:35
- Yahweh or Jehovah Sabaoth (The Lord of Hosts)—God is sovereign over everyone and everything; Isaiah 1:24; Psalm 46:7
- Yahweh or Jehovah Tsidkenu (My Righteousness)—God alone provides righteousness for mankind through Christ; Jeremiah 33:16; 2 Corinthians 5:21

If chaplains who want to research and read more on how best to minister to Christians, what would you recommend?

Spiritual care plans are generally led by patients. However, it goes without saying that the better a chaplain understands a faith group, the better soul care can be administered. Often, Christians will want the chaplain to offer biblical principles and solutions for their current life or health situations. Here's a very brief list of helpful resources to understand and minister to Christian individuals. Many great works explaining the Christian faith are available.

- Chambers, Oswald. *The Utmost for His Highest*, Grand Rapids: Discovery House, 2009.
- Clinton, Timothy, and George Ohlschlager. *Competent Christian Counseling*. Colorado Springs: Waterbrook Press, 2002.
- Clinton, Timothy, and Ron Hawkins. *Biblical Counseling: 40 Topics, Spiritual Insights and Easy-to-Use Action Steps*. Grand Rapids, 2009.
- Holloday, Tom. *The Relationship Principles of Jesus*. Grand Rapids: Zondervan, 2008.
- Holy Bible. (Specifically the Gospel of Christ as presented in the books of Matthew, Mark, Luke and John)

Conclusion

This section of *Essential Chaplain Skill Sets* has attempted to present the basic tenets and modes of spiritual expression of humanism and the primary world religions. While not exhaustive, the general concepts and spirituality of humanism, Buddhism, Hinduism, Islam, Orthodox Judaism, and Christianity were briefly reviewed.

For any chaplain ministering in a pluralistic and public environment, understanding the nuances and differences of the world religions and their expressions of spirituality will prove to be very helpful. The chaplain may not personally or theologically agree with the premises of all the belief systems discussed, but the chaplain will still afford individuals of diverse faiths the respect and understanding all of humanity is entitled to. This additional effort to understand the broad spectrum of spiritual perspectives should prove very helpful for any organizational chaplain in public ministry setting in achieving more meaningful discourse with individuals.

It is hoped that the topics and discussion in this section have been helpful in several ways. First, due to great amount of literature on these topics, I hoped to pare it down into understandable components for those new to the field of spirituality and world faiths. Secondly, my desire was to intrigue the reader to learn more and seek out the numerous references and citations listed throughout this work. And lastly, I hope that this information has given you, the reader, a solid footing in understanding the many expressions of spirituality and faith and become more comfortable in ministering to all individuals. The next section will focus on understanding the spiritual assessment.

PART 3

Understanding Spiritual Needs Assessments

CHAPTER 12

A Paradigm to Understand and Develop Emotional and Spiritual Well-Being

Before we delve into the area of spiritual assessments, I would like to pose a theoretical analogy to help determine what the chaplain wants to accomplish and possibly develop in those he or she is ministering. As a marketplace chaplain in a hospital setting and a law enforcement chaplain, I speak to many employees and officers about their life issues. The theoretical analogy I would like to present to you seems to work well. This analogy has helped me have a mental concept of how and why to establish a neutral and caring starting point for spiritual and religious conversations.

Experiencing a great quality of life involves a balance between your physical, your emotional, and your spiritual selves. The well-used analogy of a three-legged stool can be used as a visual image of what happens when one or two legs of your physical-emotional-spiritual selves are not in balance—or maybe not even present. Many people usually give their physical self the majority of attention, and the emotional self receives a very small minority of attention. This leaves, more often than not, the spiritual self totally abandoned and without any intentional nurturing.

As this triad of total holistic health becomes more balanced, each leg's strength or sphere of influence begins to overlap and strengthen the others. The greater the overlap, the stronger the triad. The stronger the triad, the greater resilience a person has when undergoing crisis and daily cumulative stress.

The diagram below shows each of the three basic legs or pillars of wellness: physical, emotional, and spiritual. Depending upon the strength of each, each one may influence and strengthen the others. Each pillar should be nurtured in equal measure and effort in order to develop great holistic wellness.

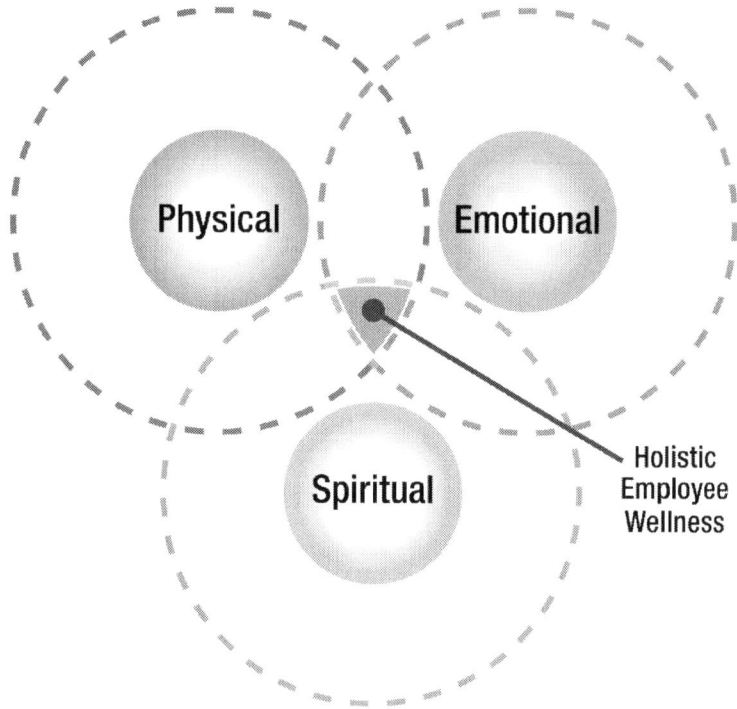

Figure 1: Holistic wellness diagram

For the remainder of this brief discussion, let's assume your physical self is well established and is the strongest leg of the three-legged stool of holistic wellness. But there remains the need to talk about the other two legs of the stool: the emotional and spiritual pillars of holistic health.

Emotional health is internally managed and directed. Your emotional health involves your learned ability to process and work through experiences and stress. How have you coped before when under stress? Were your strategies positive or negative? The stronger your emotional health becomes, the greater your ability to recover (your level of resiliency) from draining and overwhelming experiences.

As you learn what coping strategies work well for you and your personality, you learn how to emotionally respond to and manage future stressful situations more appropriately. A more practical explanation might be "your emotional health is your ability to handle emotional baggage that you pick up while doing your job and living life." When you don't possess good emotional health, you are more apt to become helplessly trapped in dark emotional states. Developing good positive ways to cope is crucial.

Spiritual health is externally directed or influenced.[101] This is your big-picture perspective of life and how you connect to nature, the divine, crisis, and even your own meaning and purpose. Spiritual health gives purpose to your human existence while guiding and developing your character, morals, integrity, and values. This area primarily involves how you interact with an external value system. Your spiritual and religious values shape your decision making (ethics) and how you base right or wrong.

Do you act and look at yourself and your work from an external perspective? It is from this external vantage point of higher, absolute values (which may be religious or not) that shape your decisions of life, relationships, work integrity, and even your view of the value or sanctity of life itself. Your spiritual health informs and guides the reasons and considerations that go into your daily decisions. People who state that they have a "calling" to do certain type of work have a spiritual perspective for what they do. In fact, they realize that even if they made much more money doing a different job, they wouldn't be truly happy not doing what they were divinely "called" to do for humanity.

But both emotional and spiritual stressors can create deep scars

---

[101] Carey A. Friedman, *Spiritual Survival for Law Enforcement* (NJ: Compass Books, 2015).

which, when not appropriately addressed, may even kill through addictions and suicide.[102] Many occupations, such as law enforcement and health-care workers, have a substantially higher risk for addictions and suicide due to the persistent daily stressors. On a grading scale of A+ to F, how would you grade your emotional self? How would you grade your spiritual self?

Let's say you work as a first responder or as an acute care health-care provider. If you only developed your physical and emotional self and ignored your spiritual self, you might probably eventually quit working in that occupation. Why? Because developing stronger physical and emotional health is wonderful, but it may not be enough for you to combat the fast-paced, cumulative stressors.

Remember, your level of *emotional health* is how you react, manage, and decide to cope (positively or negatively) to stress. Everyone has a breaking point with cumulative stress. You might be able to manage for a while, but eventually, the stressors will overwhelm you. In order to not become chronically overwhelmed, you must intentionally nurture your spirituality. Spiritual health is what inspires you and informs you about *why* you do *what* you do for others. Discover what those are for you personally. Then keep reminding yourself. This oft-ignored spiritual component is the missing link to truly living life to the fullest.

When workers go into their respected fields and begin to develop a deep inner connection (spiritual) to their jobs, they begin to understand how their efforts can dramatically influence and impact their communities and societies. Once this occurs, the spiritual awareness, energy, and inspiration of their avocation helps keep them healthy through a long career of helping others.

But without good spiritual health, you are at greater risk to develop compassion fatigue and job burnout. You may even get to the emotional breaking point and consider harming yourself or others—or even consider suicide.[103] The spiritual component is generally the

---

[102] Friedman.
[103] Kevin Gilmartin, *Emotional Survival for Law Enforcement* (E-S Press, 2002).

weakness area, and this creates the primary tipping point in the three-legged stool analogy.

Just as physical health is of critical importance for you to do your job well, completing a healthy triad by developing and maintaining a good balance in your physical, emotional, and spiritual health is of paramount importance. Don't become a physical marvel who only possesses an empty, barren soul. Become physically, emotionally, and spiritually balanced.

CHAPTER 13

What Is a Spiritual Assessment?

For chaplains in any setting, the unspoken protocol is to assess the spirituality and beliefs of the individual that they are ministering. Completing a spirituality assessment allows the chaplain to see what spiritual or faith-specific resources the individual may need for the situation. To do this well, one must understand what spirituality is and what the objectives of completing a spiritual assessment might be.

For a quick review of how spirituality is defined, Christina Puchalski, MD, of George Washington Institute of Spirituality and Health states,

> Spirituality is the aspect of humanity that refers to the way individuals seek and express meaning and purpose and the way they experience their connectedness to the moment, to self, to others, to nature, and to the significant or sacred.[104]

Stephen R. Covey states, "The spiritual dimension is your core, your center, your commitment to your value system. It's a very private area of life and a supremely important one."[105]

---

[104] Puchalski (2014), 642.

[105] Stephen R. Covey, *The 7 Habits of Highly Effective People, Signature Edition 4.0.* (Salt Lake City: Franklin Covey, date not listed), 170.

Essential Chaplain Skill Sets

One can quickly assess from just these two definitions of spirituality that spirituality is multifaceted and complex.

Chaplains are often asked, "Is there a difference between spirituality and religion?" Some may disagree, but my generalized answer is, "Yes." First of all, everyone has a spirituality within them, whether they personally recognize it or not. People are spiritual in nature. Secondly, I view religion as the way an individual or group determines how they learn and practice (rites, rituals, and worship) their spirituality, beliefs, and their theologically based faith. Religion is where your theology, doctrines, and dogmas are developed. However, I do not believe a person can commit to and authentically practice a religion without a sense of their own spirituality or spiritual needs. But one may express their spirituality outside of traditional religious practices.

George Fitchett's *Assessing Spiritual Needs: A Guide for Caregivers* (1993) has become a classic among professional chaplains and is a vital clinical pastoral education resource. Fitchett's work revealed that many approaches were being used to accomplish a spiritual assessment. He discovered that chaplains were using a broad range of spiritual assessments from informal and personal methods to very precise, impersonal "diagnostic" surveys.

Fitchett discusses the importance of the spiritual assessment. For the chaplain, the spiritual assessment becomes the foundation for developing an action plan that will direct soul care, promote intentional and effective spiritual communication, help evaluate chaplaincy interactions, maintain personal accountability and quality assurance, and establish the role and purpose of the chaplain. But whichever spiritual assessment model is used by a chaplain, these objectives should be foundational to the model's overall purpose.

Through Fitchett's research and personal experience, he developed his own spiritual assessment model called the 7×7 Model.[106] This model is conceptual, functional, and holistic and it provides a great

---

[106] George Fitchett, *Assessing Spiritual Needs: A Guide for Caregivers,* (Minneapolis: Augsburg Fortress, 1993).

framework for chaplains in any setting for spiritual assessments. In brief, he states that holistic wellness is built around seven dimensions:

- medical
- psychological
- psychosocial
- family systems
- ethnic and cultural
- societal issues
- spiritual dimensions

One can easily see the influence each of these seven dimensions has upon an individual's life and perceptions of holistic wellness.

Within the spiritual dimension, Fitchett's 7 × 7 Model describes seven smaller categories that give the broader perspective and complex intricacies for an individual's overall spirituality:

- beliefs and meaning
- vocation and consequences
- experience and emotion
- courage and growth
- ritual and practice
- community
- authority and guidance

In Douglas Edward Robinson's doctoral work on spiritual assessment and his evaluation of Fitchett's 7 × 7 Model, he states,

> For review, the two hemispheres of assessment are the Holistic and Spiritual … It is likely that you will not gain all the information you seek in the first visit, or during all of your visits. Time does not always permit this thorough an assessment. Remember that hospital patient needs and challenges can rapidly change. Hospitalized patients may present with multiple issues. When this is the case, you may first need to address the most crucial issue, before

tending to the others. The important thing to remember is that spiritual care in the hospital is need-based and fluid. Let the patient direct you to the areas in greatest need of intervention. Spiritual welfare and appropriate intervention is always more important than getting all the information. Promoting such integration requires an appropriate assessment of patient spirituality, and definition of conditions for spiritual interventions, that improve patient care.[107]

Fitchett's 7 × 7 Model seems daunting at first glance, but it actually is a commonsense and thorough approach. It hits upon all aspects of life. If a chaplain, or any person ministering to another, can remember to utilize just a few of these sections, he or she will more than likely have a meaningful encounter. Of course, the inclusion of all seven areas of the spiritual dimension remains the objective goal.

The next chapter will review a few of the more common spiritual assessments, which are in the literature and are being practically used in different clinical and public ministry settings. First, let's hear about some of the benefits of a chaplain using spiritual assessments.

The Practical Benefits of the Spiritual Assessment

Performing a spiritual assessment should not be about imposing a set of rigid questions on an individual. It should be an interactive conversation between individuals. This discussion will center on health-care settings, but the spiritual assessment can be administered in any setting with individuals who may be hurting spiritually. During a conversation with Chaplain Zac Buhuro, he said the following regarding his perspective of spiritual assessments.

Buhuro: Upon admission to the hospital, patients may undergo a spiritual screening, which is generally very short in nature. The spiritual screening simply asks questions such as, "Do you have

---

[107] Douglas Edward Robinson, "Pastoral Care: A New Model for Assessing the Spiritual Needs of Hospitalized Patients" DMin dissertation. Liberty Baptist Theological Seminary, August 2012: 111–112. www.digitalcommons.liberty.edu

spiritual beliefs? Do you have a faith or church preference? Do you want a local minister or church to visit you while you are admitted?"

However, as the patients stay for one or more days, there is a need for a professional chaplain to do the spiritual assessment. A spiritual assessment helps address the patient's needs in a more holistic way and also engages the patients on the meaning of their lives as they are dealing with an illness.

One may not claim to belong to any organized religion or even claim to be an atheist. What is important is knowing that the spiritual assessment helps taps into the core of what and who the person is in terms of making meaning of their life situation. What does it mean, for example, for a mother who is accustomed to waking up every morning, going to work, taking care of her family, and so on ... but now is in the hospital facing a serious illness? What does she make of news about a new diagnosis that may interfere with her daily life? How does she cope with that? Who supports her? How can others be of support to her?

The spiritual assessment deals with the ultimate meaning of life regardless of the person's religiosity. In my work with hospice patients, one of the dominant issues that often needed to be addressed was pain. The pain is not only physical—it is emotional, psychological, and spiritual pain. As a chaplain, I always asked patients in hospice about spiritual pain or total pain. Asking about "total pain" is a spiritual assessment question because it invites the patients to verbalize, if they are able, what their soul is going through.

Being informed that an illness can no longer be cured and that a patient may only have a few months to live can be very frightening. This information can trigger patients to conduct overall evaluations of their lives. And it is precisely in this "evaluation of life" that the patient or patient's relatives need some guiding questions of "spiritual assessment" to encourage an in-depth conversation about the meaning of life. As a chaplain, whether in an acute setting or hospice (home or hospital), it is important to address issues dealing with hope, relatedness, meaning, and forgiveness. It is very important to address a patient's deepest fears, worries, and concerns.

As a home hospice chaplain, I primarily worked in the south and west sides of Chicago. Time and time again, I found myself dealing with family dynamic issues (estrangement and forgiveness). Besides the need to make amends with others, I often encountered family members who had difficulties understanding what it means to "let go" of a loved one. As much as this is a grief issue, the one facilitating the spiritual assessment ought to look deeper because the "not letting go" can also be a guilt and forgiveness issue.

It is appropriate for a chaplain to ask forgiveness-spiritual assessment questions such as "Who may you ask forgiveness from?" or "Is there any issue or issues you need to forgive or be forgiven for?" Note that these are some of the questions to ask the patients as we do the spiritual assessment.

Another spiritual assessment question I found useful working in hospice and in inpatient units is that of meaning: For example, "Mr. Smith, I can only imagine how hard this is for you. But if I may ask you, what does this illness mean for you right now?" This question invites the patient or the patient's loved ones to talk about their beliefs, faith, family, friends, and their role in the society and in the world.

For example, if the patient was an active husband who paid all the bills, worked, and took care of his family, the "meaning-making" question is important. This is especially important if the illness will be terminal. How does the patient or family view the meaning of the illness? How has it impacted them individually, and how has the struggle of dealing with the illness or crisis changed their perspective on life and the value of relationships.

The assessment or process allows the family, the chaplain, and others to discover what might be desired in order to provide more assurance and support the well-being of the family—even after the death of their loved one. This, in turn, can bring inner peace to the patient and give them "permission" to die without worries or fears.

I strongly believe that in making the spiritual assessment, and it is also very important to ask the "relatedness" question: "Mr. Smith, what do you fear losing most?" Again, this question may open the door for the patient to talk about family relationships, work, close friends, and other meaningful aspects of life. As chaplains, what do we do with that information? The patient's sharing helps the spiritual assessor identify the needs, fears, worries, hopes, dreams, regrets, and an overall invisible metaphysical pain to help caregivers care for patients and their families in a more holistic way.

This text will review many of the current spiritual assessment models. Was there a specific one that your previous hospice organization chose for their chaplains to utilize?

Buhuro: The group I was with did not mandate the use of any one specific model. Most often, the chaplains—knowing the general concepts and principles of common spiritual assessment models—would simply include open-ended questions about the individual's beliefs and spirituality while having a calm conversation.

My objective of a spiritual assessment "conversation" is to discover as much as possible about the beliefs of the individual (and family). Are they exhibiting signs of anxiety, grief, or fear? If so, these emotions are often associated with unresolved issues of guilt, shame, forgiveness, and unfinished business with broken relationships. There can be a great deal of psychological overlap in spiritual issues. While not trying to be a psychologist, the chaplain can discover if spiritual distress or theological influences are affecting the patients.

Once the spiritual assessment conversation concludes, I would write up a spiritual report or a chaplaincy plan for the individual to be included with their overall health-care treatment plan. The plan would often include requesting that the pastor or priest come and administer specific religious practices such as Communion, common prayers, or well-known Scripture readings. It might be as simple as making sure family and social support are present for the individuals so they do not feel alone or uncared for during their health issue and convalescence.

The chaplain spiritual care plan might also include intentional follow-up conversations to help patients dissect the reasons behind their guilt, shame, and relationship issues. Of course, this is respectfully done with their permission. Helping the patient and family members to emotionally and spiritually process what is occurring with the patient is a primary component of what clinical chaplains do. The spiritual assessment is the primary tool to glean the proper information.

Chaplain Buhuro, you served as a home hospice chaplain in the Chicago area. Would you mind sharing a few specific case examples that you remember, which demonstrate the benefit of performing a spiritual assessment?

Buhuro: One case involved Mr. Gonzalez. He had just arrived from Mexico and was a very strong Catholic and the patriarch of the family. He was diagnosed with end-stage prostate cancer. The patient was informed that he had two to three months to live. He was admitted to our hospice program. A day after his admission, I visited him at home with his family.

By asking him about his biggest worries and fears, Mr. Gonzalez shared his feelings of gratitude to God and his family. He also shared his deep faith and the meaning of the illness for him through the spiritual perspective of Christ's suffering.

In my presence, he asked to talk with his wife, children, and grandchildren (in the spirit of prayers), and he thanked them personally and asked for forgiveness. A lot of tears were shed, but there also was a deep sense of peace that was the product of that emotional encounter because Mr. Gonzalez assured his family that he was going to his eternal home and that he was at peace with his God and himself. The family was very thankful for my presence and assistance. Two days later, Mr. Gonzalez died a peaceful death.

This is just one example to demonstrate how important the spiritual assessment is in these situations. Often the spiritual assessment will take the patient and family to where they would never imagine going but wanted to be all along. Leading these types of crucial conversations and open discussion about beliefs and life situations can be very beneficial for patients and their families.

Do you have some favorite texts related to spiritual assessments and the benefits of spirituality and faith upon individual's overall wellness?

(This compilation of titles is broad, going well beyond strictly spiritual assessment but also to why spiritual assessments are needed and the impact spirituality has upon an individual's life. They are not all specifically religious or faith-based texts, but they address the interacting intricacies of the psychological, emotional, and spiritual.)

- Capps, Donald. *Reframing: A New Method in Pastoral Care.* Minneapolis: Augsburg Fortress Press, 1990.
- Edmiston, John. *Biblical EQ: A Christian Handbook for Emotional Transformation.* 2001.
- Friedman, Cary A. *Spiritual Survival for Law Enforcement: Practical Insights, Practical Tools.* Linden, NJ: Compass Books, 2005.
- Lipton, Bruce H. *The Biology of Belief: Unleashing the Power of Consciousness, Matter & Miracles.* Carlsbad: Hay House, 2008.
- McSherry, Wilfred, and Linda Ross, eds. *Spiritual Assessment in Healthcare Practice.* London: M & K Publishing, 2010.
- Myss, Caroline, and C. Norman Shealy. *The Creation of Health: The Emotional, Psychological, and Spiritual Responses That Promote Health and Healing.* New York: Three Rivers Press, 1998.
- Pargament, Kenneth I. *Spiritually Integrated Psychotherapy: Understanding and Addressing the Sacred.* New York: Guilford Press, 2007.
- Pargament, Kenneth I. *The Psychology of Religion and Coping: Theory, Research and Practice.* New York: Guilford Press, 2001.

- Richardson, Ronald W. *Becoming a Healthier Pastor: Family Systems Theory and the Pastor's Own Family.* Minneapolis: Augsburg Fortress Press, 2005.
- Rother, Steve. *Spiritual Psychology: The Twelve Primary Life Lessons.* Las Vegas: Lightworker Publications, 2004.
- Stone, Howard W., and James O. Duke. *How to Think Theologically*, 2nd ed. Minneapolis: Augsburg Fortress Press, 2006.
- VandeCreek, Larry, and Arthur M. Lucas, eds. *The Discipline for Pastoral Care Giving: Foundations for Outcome Oriented Chaplaincy.* New York: Haworth Press, 2001.

CHAPTER 14

Spiritual Assessment Models

It goes without saying that most spiritual assessment models have been developed within and for clinical settings. However, chaplains in any setting can use these principles to assist their ministries.

In November 2008, the Joint Commission for Hospital Accreditation issued a general statement regarding "spiritual assessment."[108] A question was posed: "Does the joint commission specify what needs to be included in a spiritual assessment?" The commission's answer: "No. Your organization would define the content and scope of spiritual and other assessments and the qualifications of the individual(s) performing the assessment." For joint commission-accredited hospitals, spiritual assessments are recommended for the holistic health care of patients. However, the joint commission does not state who or how it is to be performed. The joint commission only recommends that it is available.

The commission presents several "[e]xamples of elements that could be, but are not required in a spiritual assessment." The elements should include the following questions directed to the patient or his/her family:

- Who or what provides the patient with strength and hope?
- Does the patient use prayer in his or her life?

---

[108] www.jointcommission.org

- How does the patient express his or her spirituality?
- How would the patient describe his or her philosophy of life?
- What type of spiritual/religious support does the patient desire?
- What is the name of the patient's clergy, minister, chaplain, pastor, or rabbi?
- What does suffering mean to the patient?
- What does dying mean to the patient?
- What are the patient's spiritual goals?
- Is there a role of church/synagogue in the patient's life?
- How does your faith help the patient cope with illness?
- How does the patient keep going day after day?
- What helps the patient get through this health-care experience?
- How has illness affected the patient and his or her family?

The following is a review of just four spiritual assessment tools (direct method, FACT, FICA, HOPE, and SPIRIT). There are more in the literature. As you read through these, you will see common themes within each. The FACT model was specifically designed for chaplains, and the other tools that will be reviewed were designed for physicians and other health-care providers (chaplains included).

The Direct Method

Stoll presented a "direct method" of spiritual assessment for health-care providers, outlining four primary areas.[109]

Concept of God or Deity. This examines theistic elements as well as religious elements.

- Is religion or God significant to you?
- Is prayer helpful to you?
- What happens when you pray?

---

[109] Ruth Stoll, *Guidelines for Spiritual Assessment*, 1979; also in McSherry, W., and Linda Ross. *Spiritual Assessment in Healthcare Practice*. London: M & K Publishing, 2010.

Sources of Hope and Strength. These relate to sources of support, particularly surrounding people and relationships.

- Who is the most important person to you?
- To whom do you turn when you need help?

Religious Practices. These address the impact that an illness might have on the patient's ability to maintain religious practices.

- Do you feel that your faith (religion) is helpful to you?
- Are there any religious practices that are important to you?

Relationship between Spiritual Beliefs and Health. This explores existential issues about the patient's concerns or visions for the future.

- What has bothered you most about being sick or about what is happening to you?
- What do you think is going to happen to you?

Ruth Stoll's direct method spiritual evaluation tool may be one of the original spiritual assessment models produced for health-care providers seeking more holistic evaluation of their patients. A weakness of Stoll's work is that it may indeed be too "direct." Wilfred McSherry writes,

> [T]hese questions appear intrusive and intimidating ... and only apply to those individuals with a religious belief and faith" but later states, "she [Stoll] indicates that there is a need for flexibility and adaptability when using the guidance and emphasizes that the assessment should always be led by the patient. Her work was developed within the USA where attitudes toward religious belief and practices are different from those in other parts of the world such as the UK.
>
> Therefore, the idea that such a model can be transferred and used without any adaptation or modification without

other religions of the world is questionable. Stoll probably did not have this in mind as she was developing guidance for use in the USA ... Despite this criticism, Stoll's work has made a significant contribution to the development of spiritual assessment tools, offering a simple framework that enables nurses to engage with patients' spiritual needs.[110]

The FACT Spiritual Assessment Model

Mark LaRocca-Pitts developed this spiritual history tool with the professional chaplain in mind, following Harold Koenig's five criteria of brevity, memorability, appropriateness, patient-centeredness, and credibility. This tool's developer states,

> Any properly trained health care practitioner can use the FACT spiritual assessment tool. This tool includes a short history with three questions (faith, availability, and coping) plus an outcome (treatment). It can form part of a larger clinical intervention, such as the physician's history and physical, a nursing admission assessment, a more in-depth chaplaincy assessment (see below), or it can be used as a stand-alone intervention.
>
> This tool is most effective when used conversationally, instead of as a checklist. The FACT spiritual assessment tool is a hybrid tool (three parts spiritual history and one part assessment) that is designed for an acute care setting (it is short and easy, versatile, and focused). A spiritual history obtains information on a person's spiritual life, history, and practices and on how these affect his or her ability to cope with the present health care crisis, which the first three questions of FACT address.
>
> A spiritual assessment involves an informed judgment concerning treatment options based on the spiritual history, which the last question of FACT addresses.

---

[110] Wilford McSherry and Linda Ross, *Spiritual Assessment in Healthcare Practice,* (London: M & K Publishing, 2010), Chapter 4.

Among these treatment options, one involves a referral to a professional chaplain for a more in-depth spiritual assessment. Faith or spirituality is a fact in the lives of many people. It is also a fact that many people use their faith or spirituality to help them cope with a health crisis.

Finally, it is arguably a fact that a person's faith or spiritual practice affects their medical outcomes. The FACT spiritual assessment tool provides a quick and accurate determination of whether or not a person's current health crisis is affecting his or her spiritual well-being, and then based on that determination, it suggests a treatment plan.[111]

F: Faith and/or Belief

- Do you have a faith background?
- Are you active in a community of faith? Ask questions and see how the patient responds. Do their spiritual and/or religious beliefs impact their current situation?

A: Active (and/or Available, Accessible, Applicable)

- Are you active in your faith?
- Do you have access to what you need to apply your faith or beliefs?

C: Coping (and/or Comfort)
Conflict (and/or Concern)

- How does your faith help them cope with your current situation?
- Do your beliefs provide you comfort in light of your problem?
- Do you have concerns that I can help you with?

---

[111] Mark LaRocca-Pitts, "FACT: Taking a spiritual history in a clinical setting" *Journal of Health Care Chaplaincy*, 2009; Vol 15, no 1:1–12. www.professionalchaplains.org

T: Treatment

- How is the individual coping?
- Does he or she need support and encouragement?
- Do he or she need more spiritual/religious resources?

Treatment might consist of specific religious/spiritual conversations, referrals for religious practices, rites (e.g., Communion or sacraments), and other faith-based needs.

LaRocca-Pitts gives general guidelines when taking a spiritual history:

- Faith is already a fact affecting the lives and health-care choices for many patients, and most already utilize practices as complementary treatment modalities: health-care professionals need to assess how it impacts their treatment choices.
- A spiritual history is not about what a person believes—it is about how faith or belief functions as a coping mechanism.
- Respect the privacy of patients with regard to spirituality—do not impose your own beliefs.
- Make referrals to professional chaplains, spiritual counselors, and community resources as appropriate.
- Your own spirituality can positively affect the clinician-patient relationship. Remember: "Cure sometimes; relieve often; comfort always." Addressing spiritual concerns with your patients can provide comfort. In itself, it is a therapeutic intervention.

The FICA Spiritual Assessment Model

Medical internist Puchalski developed this FICA spiritual history tool to help physicians and other health-care professionals address spiritual issues with patients. This tool can be used anytime during patient care, initial, follow-up visits, or as appropriately needed.[112]

F: Faith and Belief

- Do you consider yourself spiritual or religious?
- Is spirituality something that is important to you?
- Do you have spiritual beliefs that help you cope with stress/difficult times?
- What gives your life meaning?

I: Importance

- What importance does your spirituality have in your life?
- Has your spirituality influenced how you take care of yourself (your health)?
- Does your spirituality influence you in your health-care decision making (advance directives, treatment, etc.)?

C: Community

- Are you part of a spiritual community? Communities such as churches, temples, and mosques, or a group of like-minded friends, family, or yoga can serve as strong support systems for some patients.
- Does this support you? How?
- Is there a group of people you really love or who are important to you?

---

[112] Christina Puchalski and A. L. Romer, "Taking a spiritual history allows clinicians to understand patients more fully," *J Pall Med* 2000; 3:129–37. More information can be discovered at George Washington Institute of Spirituality and Health. www.gwish.edu and Spiritual Competency Resource Center www.spiritualcompentency.com

A: Address in Care

- How would you like me, your health-care provider, to address these issues in your health care?

Puchalski offers recommendations to health-care providers taking a patient's spiritual history. These are posted on the GWISH website:

- Consider spirituality as a potentially important component of every patient's physical well-being and mental health.
- Address spirituality at each complete physical examination and continue addressing it at follow-up visits if appropriate. In patient care, spirituality is an ongoing issue.
- Respect a patient's privacy regarding spiritual beliefs—don't impose your beliefs on others.
- Make referrals to chaplains, spiritual directors, or community resources as appropriate.
- Be aware that your own spiritual beliefs will help you personally and will overflow in your encounters with those for who you care to make the doctor-patient encounter a more humanistic one.

Of great importance to better ensure that spiritual assessments are not another checklist to complete, it is wise for providers to self-reflect upon their own spirituality and beliefs. Puchalski provides a tool called FICA for Self-Assessment. In essence, the FICA questions are simply restated in a first-person voice for the reader to personally answer.

F: Faith and Belief

- Do I have a spiritual belief that helps me cope with stress?
- Do I have a spiritual belief that helps me cope with illness?
- What gives my life meaning?

I: Importance

- Is this belief important to me?
- Does it influence how I think about my health and illness?
- Does it influence my health-care decisions?

C: Community

- Do I belong to a spiritual community (church, temple, mosque, or another group)?
- Am I happy there?
- Do I need to do more with the community?
- Do I need to search for another community?
- If I don't have a community, would it help me if I found one?

A: Address in Care

- What should my action plan be?
- What changes do I need to make?
- Are there spiritual practices I want to develop?
- Would it help for me to see a chaplain, spiritual director, or pastoral counselor?

The HOPE Spiritual Assessment Model

The HOPE questionnaire for spiritual assessment was initially developed to help medical students and practicing physicians assess patients in a more holistic manner.[113]

The H of the mnemonic pertains to the patient's basic spiritual resources without immediately focusing upon religious or spirituality. The O and P refer to areas of inquiry about the importance of organized religion in the patient's life. The E pertains to the effects

---

[113] Gowri Anandarajah and Ellen Hight, "Spirituality and Medical Practice: Using the HOPE Questions as a Practical Tool for Spiritual Assessment" *Am Fam Physician* January 1, 2001; 63(1):81–89.

of the patients' spirituality and beliefs upon their medical care and end-of-life issues.

The following description of the HOPE mnemonic with example questions originated from table 4 of the author's published work.

H: Sources of Hope (Comfort, Strength, Peace, Love, and Connection)

- We have been discussing your support systems. I was wondering, what is there in your life that gives you internal support?
- What are your sources of hope, strength, comfort, and peace?
- What do you hold on to during difficult times?
- What sustains you and keeps you going?
- For some people, their religious or spiritual beliefs act as a source of comfort and strength in dealing with life's ups and downs; is this true for you?
- If the answer is yes, go on to O and P questions.
- If the answer is no, consider asking: "Was it ever?" If the answer is yes, ask: "What changed?"

O: Organized Religion

- Do you consider yourself part of an organized religion?
- How important is this to you?
- What aspects of your religion are helpful and not so helpful to you?
- Are you part of a religious or spiritual community?
- Does it help you? How?

P: Personal Spirituality/Practices

- Do you have personal spiritual beliefs that are independent of organized religion? What are they?
- Do you believe in God?
- What kind of relationship do you have with God?

- What aspects of your spirituality or spiritual practices do you find most helpful to you personally (prayer, meditation, reading Scripture, attending religious services, listening to music, hiking, communing with nature)?

E: Effects on medical care and end-of-life issues

- Has being sick (or your current situation) affected your ability to do the things that usually help you spiritually? Has it affected your relationship with God?
- As a doctor, is there anything I can do to help you access the resources that usually help you?
- Are you worried about any conflicts between your beliefs and your medical situation/care/decisions?
- Would it be helpful for you to speak to a clinical chaplain/ community spiritual leader?

The SPIRIT Spiritual Assessment Model

The SPIRIT spiritual history tool was designed for palliative care and end-of-life providers. In the abstract, Maugans writes, "Spirituality can be defined as a belief system focusing on intangible elements that impart vitality and meaning to life's events … Spiritual belief systems impact on the incidences, experiences, and outcomes of several common medical problems."[114]

S: Spiritual Belief System

- Do you have a religious affiliation? Can you describe this?
- Do you have a spiritual life that is important to you?
- What is the clearest sense of the meaning of your life at this time?

---

[114] T. A. Maugans, "The SPIRITual history" *Arch Fam Med* 1996; Vol 5, Issue 1:11–16.

P: Personal Spirituality

- Describe the beliefs and practices of your religion that you personally accept personal spirituality.
- Describe those beliefs and practices that you do not accept or follow.
- In what ways is your spirituality/religion important to you?
- How is your spirituality important to you in everyday life?

I: Integration with a Spiritual Community

- Do you belong to any religious or spiritual groups or communities?
- How do you participate in this group/community?
- What is your role?
- What importance does this group have for you?
- In what ways is this group a source of support for you?
- What types of support and help does this group provide for you in dealing with health issues?

R: Ritualized Practices and Restrictions

- What specific practices do you carry out as part of your religious and spiritual life (e.g., prayer, meditation, services, etc.)?
- What lifestyle activities or practices does your religion encourage, discourage, or forbid?
- What meaning do these practices and restrictions have for you? To what extent have you followed these guidelines?

I: Implications for Medical Care

- Are there specific elements of medical care that your religion discourages or forbids?
- To what extent have you followed these guidelines?

- What aspects of your religion/spirituality would you like to keep in mind as I care for you?
- What knowledge or understanding would strengthen our relationship as physician and patient?
- Are there barriers to our relationship based upon spiritual or religious issues?
- Would you like to discuss the religious or spiritual implications of health care?

T: Terminal Event Planning

- Are there particular aspects of medical care that you wish to forgo or have withheld because of your religion/spirituality?
- Are there religious or spiritual practices or rituals that you would like to have available in the hospital or at home?
- Are there religious or spiritual practices that you wish to plan for at the time of death or following death?
- For what in your life do you still feel gratitude even though ill?
- When you are afraid or in pain, how do you find comfort?
- As we plan for your medical care near the end of life, in what ways will your religion or spirituality influence your decisions?

To summarize, as you review and reread through these popular and well-used spiritual history assessment tools, you will recognize common themes in the surveys. A spiritual assessment can be very structured, formal, and robotic in nature. Hopefully, it will be more personal, informal, and conversational. The other party is often unaware that the chaplain is conducting a spiritual assessment since the patient is participating in a deep and meaningful conversation.

CHAPTER 15

Workplace Spirituality Measurement Tools

By far, most spiritual assessments are geared toward individuals in clinical settings and are performed by health-care workers and chaplains. The following section reviews assessment survey tools that may be considered when chaplains or business leaders desire to spiritually assess a group or even an entire organization. Doing such may give the chaplaincy department more organizational information to guide their own ministry or department initiatives for new internal services to staff and peers.

This section adapts and adds to conceptual theories proposed by Robert A. Giacalone, Carole J. Jurkiewicz, and Louis W. Fry, as well as work by David W. Miller and Timothy Ewest, in classifying various spirituality scales. Most scales represented have been categorized as manifestation scales by Miller and Ewest.

Based upon a theological premise that professional chaplains should use more neutral language that fits to the current culture of their workplace, a problem now arises for organizations and chaplains in deciding which spirituality measurement tool best fits both secular and religiously pluralistic settings.

This chapter will familiarize you with the commonly used spirituality survey measurement tools that have been published. For executive and business leaders, this chapter will also review David Miller's workplace spirituality tool called the "Integration Box."

A cursory review of primary spiritual assessment surveys that have predominantly been used and suggested in the last three decades of qualitative research literature is annotated below by year, developer, what the scale measures, publication reference, and abstract (if available). The scales to be reviewed will be the following:

- Spiritual Well-Being Scale (1982)
- Duke Religion Index (1997)
- Brief Multidimensional Measure of Religiousness and Spirituality (1999)
- Spirituality at Work (2000)
- Spirit at Work Scale (2006)
- The Integration Box (2007)
- The 3H and BMEST Models (2008)
- Spiritual Climate Inventory (2009)
- Faith at Work Scale (2009)

The following is strictly a cursory overview and not an in-depth analysis of each spiritual assessment survey. For readers interested in a deeper understanding of what each survey provides, reference citations are included. After this cursory overview, a more detailed analysis of David Miller's Integration Box survey will be given.

Spiritual Well-Being Scale[115]
Year: 1982

Scale evaluates a global measure of people's perception of their spiritual well-being.
Special note: A 1991 evaluation of the SWBS noted,

---

[115] Raymond F. Paloutzian and C. W. Ellison. "Loneliness, Spiritual Well-Being and Quality of Life." In *Loneliness: A Sourcebook of Current Theory, Research and Therapy*. Editors L. A. Peplau and D. Perlman, (New York: Wiley, 1982), 224–37.

Test-retest and internal consistency reliability coefficients and descriptive data for several religious, student, and client groups who were administered the Spiritual Well-Being Scale developed by R. F. Paloutzian and C. W. Ellison (1982).

Because of ceiling effects, in evangelical samples, the typical respondent received the maximum score; thus, the scale was not useful in distinguishing among individuals for purposes such as selection of spiritual leaders. The scale is useful for research and as a global index of lack of well-being.[116]

Duke Religion Index[117]
Year: 1997

Scale evaluates organizational or non-organizational religion and intrinsic religiosity.

Abstract: The Duke Religion Index is a five-item scale that captures three major dimensions of religiousness: the organizational, non-organizational, and subjective or intrinsic religiosity dimensions. The first two items were taken from large community and clinical studies conducted in North Carolina. The final three items were extracted from Hoge's ten-item intrinsic religiosity scale. The resulting index captures three dimensions of religiousness that are related in overlapping yet unique ways to social support and different health outcomes.

---

[116] Rodger K. Bufford, Raymond F. Paloutzian, and Craig W. Ellison, "Norms for the Spiritual Well-Being Scale." *Journal of Psychology and Theology* 19, no. 1 (1991): 56–70. www.psychnet.apa.org.

[117] Harold G. Koenig, George R. Parkerson, Jr. and Keith G. Meador, "Religion Index for Psychiatric Research" *The American Journal of Psychiatry*, 154, no 6 (June 1997): 885–886.

Brief Multidimensional Measure of Religiousness/Spirituality[118]
Year: 1999

Scale evaluates the religious and spiritual.
  Special note: A separate study by Johnstone was conducted on the BMMRS in 2009:

Rationale. This study attempted to differentiate statistically the spiritual and religious factors of the Brief Multi-Dimensional Measure of Religiousness/Spirituality (BMMRS), which was developed based on theoretical conceptualizations that have yet to be adequately empirically validated in a population with significant health disorders.

Participants. One hundred sixty-four individuals with heterogeneous medical conditions [i.e., brain injury, spinal cord injury (SCI), cancer, stroke, primary care conditions].

Methods. Participants completed the BMMRS as part of a pilot study on spirituality, religion, and physical and mental health.

Results. A principal component factor analysis with varimax rotation and Kaiser normalization identified a six-factor solution (opposed to the expected eight-factor solution) accounting for 60 percent of the variance in scores, labeled as:

- positive spiritual experience
- negative spiritual experience
- forgiveness
- religious practices
- positive congregational support
- negative congregational support

---

[118] Fetzer Institute. "Multidimensional measurement of religiousness/spirituality for use in health research" Bethesda: Fetzer Institute, *National Institute of Aging* (1999): 1–95.

Conclusions. The results suggest the BMMRS assesses distinct positive and negative aspects of religiousness and spirituality that may be best conceptualized in a psycho-neuro-immunological context as measuring:

- *Spiritual Experiences* (emotional experience of feeling connected with a higher power/the universe)
- *Religious Practices* (prayer, rituals, service attendance)
- *Congregational Support*
- *Forgiveness* (a specific coping strategy that can be conceptualized as religious or nonreligious in context)[119]

Spirituality at Work[120]
Year: 2000

Scale evaluates inner life, meaningful work, and community.

Abstract: There is increasing evidence that a major transformation is occurring in many organizations. In what is sometimes referred to as the *spirituality movement*, organizations that have long been viewed as rational systems are considering making room for the spiritual dimension, a dimension that has less to do with rules and order and more to do with meaning, purpose, and a sense of community (*USA Today, BusinessWeek, Wall Street Journal*). Yet, we still know very little about this spiritual phenomenon. In this article, we offer a conceptualization and definition of spirituality at work and present empirical support for a measure of it.

---

[119] Brick Johnstone, Dong Pil Yoon, Kelly Lora Franklin, Laura Schopp, and Joseph Hinkebein, "Re-conceptualizing the factor structure of the Brief Multidimensional Measure of Religiousness/Spirituality" *Journal of Religion and Health* 48, no. 2 (2009): 146–63. www.jstor.org.

[120] Donde P. Ashmos and Dennis Duchon, "Spirituality at Work. A Conceptualization and Measure." *Journal of Management Inquiry*, 9, no. 2 (2000): 134–45.

Chaplain Keith Evans

Spirit at Work Scale (SWS)[121]
Year: 2006

Scale evaluates engaging work, sense of community, spiritual connection, and mystical experience.

Abstract: The Spirit at Work Scale (SAWS) is a new eighteen-item measure assessing the experience of spirituality at work. Three hundred and thirty-three employees of a large Midwestern university, ranging in occupations from the trades through senior administration, responded to a 102-item instrument assessing aspects of spirit at work.

Factor analyses revealed four distinct factors: engaging work, sense of community, spiritual connection, and mystical experience. Using the results of item analyses and factor analyses, eighteen items were selected to constitute the new scale. Analyses reveal high internal consistency for both the total scale ($\alpha =\_93$) and the four subscales (α's from_86 to_91). There was no relationship between SAWS scores and age, gender, education, or income. However, SAWS scores were related to occupation and marital status.

Management and professional staff reported significantly higher levels of spirit at work than did administrative, clerical, technical, or trade staff. Individuals who were separated, divorced, or widowed reported more spirit at work than those individuals who were single. Significant relationships between some demographic factors and some of the subscales were also found. SAWS is a short, psychometrically sound, and easy-to-administer measure that holds much promise for use in research and practice.

---

[121] Val Kinjerski and Berna J. Skrypnek, "Measuring the Intangible: Development of the Spirit at Work Scale" in *Best Paper Proceedings of the Sixty-fifth Annual Meeting of the Academy of Management* (CD). Editor M. Weaver. (2006): A1–A6; also Kinjerski, Val, and Berna J. Skrypnek. "A Human Ecological Model of Spirit at Work." *Journal of Management, Spirituality & Religion* 3, no. 3 (2006): 232–39. www.proceedings.aom.org.

The Integration Box[122]
Year: 2007

Scale evaluates ethics, experience, expression, and enrichment.

Abstract: The subject under study is the "Faith at Work" movement. Our thesis is that a complex set of variables emerged in the 1980s that, taken together, gave rise to a bona fide social movement that we call the Faith at Work (FAW) movement. This largely lay-founded and lay-led movement formed outside the church and the academy. We argue that this movement is of significant theological, ecclesiastical, ethical, and social importance. To facilitate further analysis of the movement, we propose a typology called the Integration Box.

The presenting problem for many in the FAW movement is a profound disconnection that workers and business professionals experience between Sunday worship and Monday work. We call this the Sunday-Monday gap. Tired of living bifurcated lives, yet convinced that their work matters to God, laypeople are gathering in various groups and forums to discover ways to integrate their faith and work. As such, the organizing principle of the movement is a quest to integrate faith and work.

After studying the theological and sociological contours of the movement's twentieth-century antecedent roots, we investigate the current movement. Drawing on and analyzing quantitative and qualitative evidence of the FAW movement qua movement, we identify the key contextual variables shaping and driving the movement, investigate the response of the academy and the church, and perform a detailed theological and social analysis of the various participants, forms, groups, and modes of expression that comprise the FAW movement.

In response to our analysis and findings, we offer a constructive new framework and language to better understand, discuss,

---

[122] David W. Miller, *God at Work: The History and Promise of the Faith at Work Movement*. Oxford: Oxford University Press, 2007; also Miller, David W. 2003. "The Faith at Work Movement: It's Growth, Dynamics and Future," PhD diss., Princeton University. http://search.proquest.com.

analyze, and critique the FAW movement and its participants. This framework, the Integration Box, is a typology with quadrants representing the four manifestations of FAW (called "the Four Es") as well as a proposed fifth integrative type. Our study concludes with a discussion of programmatic implications and proposals for the academy, denominations, the local church, and for the FAW movement itself.

The 3 H and BMEST Models[123]
Year: 2008

Scales evaluate 3 H (head, heart, hands), BMEST (body, mind, spirit, environment, social, and transcendent) universal aspects of spirituality.
    Abstract:

Purpose: The explosion of evidence in the last decade supporting the role of spirituality in whole-person patient care has prompted proposals for a move to a biopsychosocial-spiritual model for health. Making this paradigm shift in today's multicultural societies poses many challenges, however. This article presents two theoretical models that provide common ground or further exploration of the role of spirituality in medicine.

Methods: The 3 H model (head, heart, hands) and the BMEST models (body, mind, spirit, environment, social, transcendent) evolved from the author's twelve-year experience with curricula development regarding spirituality and medicine, sixteen-year experience as an attending family physician and educator, experience with Hinduism and Christianity since childhood, and a lifetime study of the world's great spiritual traditions. The models were developed, tested with learners, and refined.

---

[123] Gowri Anandarajah, "The 3 H and BMEST Models for Spirituality in Multicultural Whole-Person Medicine" *Annals of Family Medicine* 6, no. 5 (2008) 448–58.

Results: The 3 H model offers a multidimensional definition of spirituality, applicable across cultures and belief systems that provide opportunities for a common vocabulary for spirituality. Therapeutic options, from general spiritual care (compassion, presence, and the healing relationship) to specialized spiritual care (e.g., by clinical chaplains), to spiritual self-care are discussed. The BMEST model provides a conceptual framework for the role of spirituality in the larger health-care context, useful for patient care, education, and research. Interactions among the six BMEST components—with references to ongoing research—are proposed.

Conclusions: Including spirituality in whole-person care is a way of furthering our understanding of the complexities of human health and well-being. The 3 H and BMEST models suggest a multidimensional and multidisciplinary approach based on universal concepts and a foundation in both the art and science of medicine.

Spiritual Climate Inventory[124]
Year: 2009

Scale evaluates harmony with self, harmony at work, transcendence.

Abstract: This study examines the notion of *spirituality* as a dimension of human self, and its relevance and role in management. Major thesis of this research is that spirituality of employees is reflected in work climate. This may, in turn, affect the employees' service to the customers.

In the first part of the study, a *spiritual climate inventory* is developed and validated with data from manufacturing and service sector employees. In the later part, hypothesis of positive impact of spiritual climate on customers' experience of employees' service is examined and found to be substantiated empirically.

---

[124] Ashish Pandey, Rajen K. Gupta, and A. P. Arora, "Spiritual Climate of Business Organizations and Its Impact on Customer Experience" *Journal of Business Ethics* 88, no. 2 (2009): 313–32. www.jstor.org.

Chaplain Keith Evans

Faith at Work Scale[125]
Year: 2009

Scale evaluates relationship, meaning, community, holiness, and giving.

Abstract: Workplace spirituality research has sidestepped religion by focusing on the function of belief rather than its substance. Although establishing a unified foundation for research, the functional approach cannot shed light on issues of workplace pluralism, individual or institutional faith-work integration, or the institutional roles of religion in economic activity. To remedy this, we revisit definitions of spirituality and argue for the place of a belief-based approach to workplace religion.

Additionally, we describe the construction of a fifteen-item measure of workplace religion informed by Judaism and Christianity—the Faith at Work Scale (FWS). A stratified random sample ($n = 234$) of managers and professionals assisted in refining the FWS, which exhibits a single factor structure (Eigenvalue = 8.88; variance accounted for = 59.22%) that is internally consistent (Cronbach's $\alpha = 0.77$) and demonstrates convergent validity with the Faith Maturity Scale ($r = 0.81, p > 0.0001$). The scale shows lower skew and kurtosis with Mainline and Catholic adherents than with Mormons and Evangelicals. Validation of the scale among Jewish and diverse Christian adherents would extend research in workplace religion.

---

[125] Monty L. Lynn, Michael J. Naughton, and Steve VanderVeen, "Faith at Work Scale (FWS): Justification, Development, and Validation of a Measure of Judeo-Christian Religion in the Workplace" *Journal of Business Ethics* 85, no. 2 (2009): 227–243. www.link.springer.com.

CHAPTER 16

Assessing the Spirituality of an Organization or Group

The presented spirituality assessment surveys have been categorized as manifestations scales as they "pertain to the orientation to universal, religious or spiritual values, disclosing specific manifestations, phenomenological experiences without regard to specific traditions, and expressions of a person's values and corresponding motivations."[126]

How people's spirituality and faith is manifested and informs their life is critical to their perception of their own purpose and meaning, as well as life satisfaction and emotional well-being. Identifying the appropriate workplace spirituality survey is then all the more important.

Unlike Miller's theory, most workplace spirituality theories, surveys, and scales are narrowly focused on just a single religion or a discipline-specific theory. In doing so, these definitions or concepts of spirituality "may only be accepted within specific academic guilds, thus missing the vital multivariate and interdisciplinary aspects of spiritually."[127] This is seen as reductionist and highly exclusive.

---

[126] Robert A. Giacalone, Carole J. Jurkiewicz, and Louis W. Fry, "From Advocacy to Science: The Next Steps in Workplace Spirituality Research" In *Handbook of the Psychology of Religion and Spirituality*, eds. Raymond F. Paloutzian and Crystal L. Park, (New York: Guilford Publications, 2005), 521.

[127] Giacolone et al, 521.

Scholars in this field have related that workplace spirituality scales should not only account for a personal belief (nature of spirtualty) but also should include individual relationships and outcomes.

Giacolone, Jurkiewicz, and Fry suggest that religious scales are typically "designed to assess individual adherence to theistic connection, or membership affiliation," and that workplace scales are different in that they have the challenge of measuring the "interactive relationship of organizational and personal beliefs and their impact on criterion variables." A workplace spirituality theory and model needs to be broad-based, inclusive, and multivariant.

Louis (Jody) W. Fry has conducted extensive work on spiritual leadership over the past few decades. This work has formed the Spiritual Business Leadership (SBL) survey and scorecard. Fry's method focuses on administrative and organization commitment toward spiritual leadership.

Even though the SBL survey is not religious-specific in nature, it is the opinion of this reviewer that organizations with the most strategic spiritual impact upon employees and work environments that Fry highlights appear to only arise directly from the company owners and administrators' personal spiritual and religious convictions and efforts.[128] For readers who own businesses, serve in organizational leadership, or serve as corporate chaplains, Fry and Altman's *Spiritual Leadership in Action: The CEL Story* will be an excellent resource, providing insight and ideas for how to transform an organization's spiritual culture from the top down, following Fry's Spiritual Business Scorecard.

However, one might question that if an organization's ownership or upper leadership is not specifically focused upon engaging employees in this intentional way, would the perspective of workplace spirituality improve? A new rubric for evaluating workplace spirituality may prove helpful.

---

[128] Louis W. Fry and Yochanan Altman, *Spiritual Leadership in Action: The CEL Story, Achieving Extraordinary Results through Ordinary People*. (Charlotte: Information Age Publishing, Inc. 2013).

New Organizational Rubric for Workplace Spirituality Instruments

David Miller and Timothy Ewest have presented a new organizational rubric based upon the perspective that past workplace spirituality scales and instruments have been inadequate at addressing the inherently multivariant nature of religion and spirituality. The new rubric places workplace spirituality measuring instruments into three categories: manifestation scales, development scales, and adherence scales. These are explained as follows:

Manifestation scales pertain to the orientation to universal, religious, or spiritual values, disclosing specific manifestations, phenomenological experiences without regard to specific traditions, and expressions of a person's values and corresponding motivations. Development scales pertain to the level of development within the participant in reference to a range of mature versus immature belief, and/or nascent or developed religious/spiritual expectations. Adherence scales pertain to authentic adherence of religious, spiritual, or traditional beliefs and the integration or practice of specific religious or spiritual traditions without regard to maturity.[129]

Because of the more inclusive nature of the manifestation scale classification, Miller and Ewest consider this style of scale to be the better choice for organizations to consider.

The Integration Box evaluation model holds special utility for any diverse cultural and organizational setting and produces exceptional holistic data. This model is designed to evaluate four differing areas that employees and organizations may manifest spirituality: ethics, expression, experience, and enrichment (figure 1). This manifestation scale avoids religious language and focuses upon the practical applications and ways individuals display their spirituality despite their traditional faith backgrounds or lack thereof.

---

[129] Giacalone et al, 517–518.

Chaplain Keith Evans

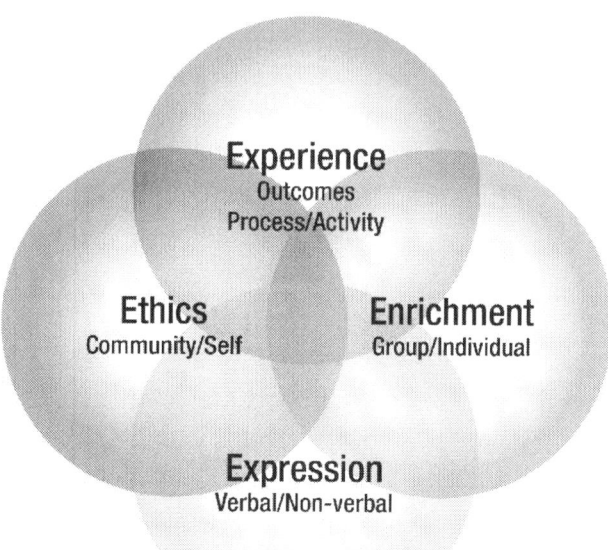

Figure 2. The Integration Box Four E's
www.princeton.edu/faithandwork

Based upon a sociology framework theory of Marco Diani, Miller's doctoral work observed that workplace spirituality theories need to possess two primary foci: a theory that (1) allows "for individuals to live holistic lives in the workplace with multiple faith perspectives," and (2) recognizes different individual behavioral ways "to integrate faith into the workplace."[130]

As FAW has continually developed, it is observed that the integration process is displayed in different ways for different people. At the core of this model is that all individuals will have a natural predisposition or learned orientation in the way they will express their spirituality and faith. They will express in one or more or the

---

[130] David W. Miller and Timothy Ewest, "The Integration Box (TIB): An Individual and Institutional Faith, Religion, and Spirituality at Work Assessment Tool" www.princeton.edu.

four manifestation types: ethics, expression, experience, and/or enrichment.[131] A brief explanation of each follows.

The Ethics Type

The ethics type places high value on attention to ethical concerns. People's spirituality and faith will guide their levels of ethical decision-making as they are guided, compelled, and inspired. For nonreligious employees, decisions will be based upon experiences, culture, and societal norms, as well as placing a high personal standard to their own ethical behaviors (negative or positive).

For the religious Christian employee, the wisdom for their decision making will be more informed and shaped by the Scriptures, biblical principles, narratives, and parables. When positively expressed, this places emphasize toward the personal virtues of integrity, character, honesty, loyalty, and respect for others. As negatively expressed, misconduct of sexual impropriety, disrespectful behavior toward others, cheating on expenses, conflicts of interest, and misuse of power might be observed.

The Expression Type

The expression type places high value on the ability to express their faith tradition and worldview to others. Whether this is by verbal or nonverbal expressions, expression is central to their identity, whether it is evangelical in nature or indirect expression by using faith symbols in jewelry, office art, etc. The purpose is for persuasion of others toward faith and spirituality, responding to a sense of obligation to express their faith and spirituality, or simply exercising their right of religious liberty.

It is the opinion of this writer that the manner in which people express their faith and spirituality at work may well be based upon their own individual personality and temperament as well as the level of openness of the organization or coworkers for employees to express themselves.

---

[131] Miller and Ewest, 5–10.

The Experience Type

The experience type places high value on how they experience their work, understanding work as a spiritual calling with special meaning and purpose. These individuals or organizations view work primarily as a means to an end. They search for meaning, purpose, and intrinsic value in the work itself. They desire to have a deep personal resonance and possibly a divine importance to their chosen work, calling, or vocation. Miller explains that this type of employee views work and occupation as a means or platform for something greater, an influential impact upon society, or in another person's life.

The Enrichment Type

The enrichment type places high value on drawing strength and comfort from religious/spiritual and/or consciousness practices. This type will seek others (groups) with similar inclinations, finding comfort, growth, and encouragement in group interactions. Their individual spirituality and faith helps them draw strength and cope with stress and pressures at work, as well as discovering wisdom and personal growth through the work process.

Miller states that this type of employee is often inward and individually contemplative in nature. They enjoy self-practices of meditation, prayer, devotional readings, scripture study, liturgical activities, accountability exercises, yoga, and other reflective practices. These practices are viewed to increase inner sustenance, healing, and personal transformation, and they are performed in order to draw closer to God, commune with the divine, or become one with the universe. These inward-oriented faith practices enrich the ability to cope and thrive in their outward-oriented work lives.

Reasons to Consider the Integration Box

There are solid reasons for an organization to consider using David Miller's the Integration Box (TIB) spirituality survey. Holistic or multidimensional theories and their accompanying psychometric scales best address the nature of spirituality (Miller and Ewest, 11). The goal of the TIB and other multidimensional theories is to help individuals understand and measure how they integrate faith and work.

Another reason is to assist organizations that wish to understand, measure, and respond constructively to the phenomena of workplace spirituality and religiously rooted values and behaviors in the workplace. Miller states, "Without such an assessment tool, managers and employees are unable to understand or identify the constructive individual and business benefits of faith at work, which often provide personal foundations and motivations for ethics, engagement, loyalty, excellence, integrity, and meaning and purpose in work (all aspects of the Four E's)."[132]

Without an instrument that identifies the more social constructs of spirituality, organizational management will be unprepared to develop policies and practices to educate and prevent abuse and misuse of workplace spirituality ... [and will also be] ill-equipped to provide appropriate protections for minority religions, and other spiritual practices, behaviors, and accommodations, as protected by law; particularly when they are unfamiliar to or misunderstood by management and the majority religious population.[133]

This theory and multidimensional assessment tool "is designed to work in pluralistic, multi-faith organizational environments where multiple spiritual orientations and identities exist."[134] The tool is based upon social, theoretical, and theological underpinnings, which allows it to have great promise for any organization to utilize in improving employee well-being, engagement, and alignment of organization values.

One may individually take the TIB survey and receive a complimentary 4E score by going to www.tibsurvey.com.

---

[132] Miller and Ewest, 15.
[133] Miller and Ewest, 15.
[134] Miller and Ewest, 15–16.

PART 4

Bringing the Pieces Together

CHAPTER 17

Bringing the Pieces Together

A lot has been covered regarding the why, what, who, and how of chaplaincy. Let's now attempt to bring most of it together and observe various chaplain encounters. These six examples are from a hospital clinical setting, but you will note that these conversations could have easily occurred in any setting. Chaplain encounters will happen anywhere.

The written-out form of a chaplain encounter is called a *verbatim*. A verbatim is a method used in clinical pastoral education (CPE) to train chaplains on the many nuances of an encounter. The key elements of the verbatim include observation, psychological, and theological reflection, social and cultural concerns, and personal meaning. In the CPE setting, the verbatim is presented before chaplain peers who offer constructive critique.

Throughout the verbatim, you will notice many parenthetical statements within the dialogue. The parentheticals reveal the self-awareness of the chaplains regarding their own emotions or thoughts, as well as where they feel the conversation may be leading or should be lead. At the end of the dialogue, the chaplains present their own self-analysis of various aspects of what they sensed was occurring with the patient as well as identifying new areas for learning. All references to the actual chaplain's or patient's names have been changed. As you read these, you may agree or not agree with how the chaplain proceeded with the encounter. That is good.

If you are studying this text with a group, you might consider discussing how you might have approached the encounter differently regarding aspects of culture, existential, spiritual, and behavioral issues. Following each verbatim are additional questions that came to my mind for you to consider as well. As you read, try to place yourself in that setting. Take notes on what other possible ways you may have asked different open-ended questions or offered other restatements, theological reflections, or social/cultural assessments.

VERBATIM 1

Headaches

Known Facts

Per the daily patient census, I know that "Hope" is a sixty-six-year-old female who stated her religious preference as nondenominational. She was admitted to a double room the night before and was placed in the bed nearest the window across the room.

Pastoral Plan

My general pastoral plan for an initial patient visit is to create an open environment for conversation and spiritual dialogue as the patient allows. This dialogue will be prompted by my questions about their spirituality and their current concerns. One primary objective of my initial visit with admitted patients is to meet them and make sure they understand that they can feel free to contact the chaplain's office and request any form of spiritual care. The office will do everything in its power to fulfill those wishes through our own chaplains or by contacting outside ministers to come to the hospital. Another primary objective of the initial visit is to assess the patient's spirituality and offer spiritual/religious support through dialogue and/or prayer as appropriate for the situation.

Chaplain Keith Evans

Description of the Patient and Setting

Hope is in a double room with her bed by the window. Her curtain was drawn around her bed. I first visited briefly with the patient in the first bed and two family members who were present. As I was talking with them, I could hear Hope moaning and moving around in her bed on the other side of the curtain. I also noticed that this patient's IV machine was beeping loudly.

The Visit

C1: Good morning. I'm _____. I'm a chaplain with the hospital. Are you Hope? (Patient nods.) I wanted to stop by and introduce myself to see if there was anything that I or the chaplain's office may do for you today. How are you doing?
(Patient is moving in her bed and has her right arm flexed up and over her head, rubbing the back of her head. She is maintaining good eye contact and begins shifting her body in the bed toward my direction as though she is willing and wanting to hold a conversation.)
P1: I've got an intense migraine that started yesterday. That beeping noise is killing me! (She motions her head toward the monitor next to her.)
C2: I'm sure that must be very annoying. May I shut the window blinds or anything for you? Are you having any visual sensitivity with your headache?
P2: No, thank you. It is mainly that constant noise. They gave me medication for the migraine, but it has only cut the edge off a little. My head still hurts.
C3: Did you come to the hospital last night?
P3: Yes. My migraine headache would not let up over the past three days. I asked my daughter to take me, but she was too busy, so I drove myself.
C4: Is it just you at home alone?

P4: I live at a senior living facility. I am divorced and have three grown daughters. Two of them live out of town, but the youngest one, who is twenty-seven years old, is still around. She just had a little baby and does not come visit me anymore. I called her last night, and she did not have time for me. (Patient continues to rub her temples as she thinks about her daughter not bringing her to the hospital last night.)

C5: So your daughter could not drive you last night because of her infant? (I am trying to clarify and restate her comments.)

P5: Yes. Her baby is six months old. The doctors think many of my headaches are brought on by my stress. I get stressed a lot when thinking about my kids. I came to the ER last night, and they admitted me this morning.

C6: So there was not anyone else home to drive you here? (Why did I ask that? Didn't I just ask her that?)

P6: I know a lot of people there, but most don't like me much. They think of me as a Holy

Roller.

C7: Why is that?

P7: I don't drink, and I read my Bible. I pray and go to church every week. They tend to insult me or make little wisecracks all the time.

C8: It sounds like you have a strong faith, a faith like the apostle Paul's, who faced all sorts of insults and even physical abuse for his faith in Christ. He had lots of trials in his life. (I believe that theological reflection flows well!)

P8: Yes. I'm encouraged by the life of Paul. I was raised in a Baptist church by my parents and have been involved for most of my life. I'm not perfect, but I do try the best I can. Could you pray for me and my family?

C9: I would be delighted and honored to do so, Hope. What specifically should I pray about? (I ask this to solicit her needs more and to not simply assume what her primary concerns are for the moment.)

P9: Please pray that my headache will go away. Pray for my daughters and that they will be more involved with a church. They have drifted away and do not go anymore.

C10: Is there anything else?

P10: No. That is all I need right now.

C11: Let's pray then. Dear Heavenly Father, You are the most high and majestic Creator of nature and all of life. We are bowing our heads before you in honor and reverence as we ask your presence this morning. You are the great Jehovah Jireh, the Provider, and wonderful Jehovah Rapha, our Healer. We ask for your hand of grace and mercy upon Hope. Please give her the perseverance to endure her headache until it can be calmed, and I do ask that you bless her with comfort and rest. Allow her to sense your presence and to know that she is in your protective hands. We also pray for her health-care team, her nurses, and her physicians, so that they have wisdom and discernment in discovering what exactly is causing her headaches. Lord, we ask for your grace and mercy upon her daughters. Please continue to direct them in the way of your will and encourage them toward righteousness and lives that will be pleasing to you, Lord. All this we humbly pray. Amen.

P11: Thank you for coming by and praying for me. God bless you.

(I said my farewell and delight in meeting her and reminded her to simply ask her nurse to contact us if she needs anything further from the chaplain's office.)

Interpretation and Evaluation

Assessment of the Person

Hope is a talkative lady who is openly expressive of her needs and concerns. We connected quickly, and she reached out in requesting prayer relatively early in our conservation.

Psychological Concerns

It was apparent to me that Hope wanted affirmation that her headaches were real and that someone cares about her physical suffering. She also quickly expressed her faith tradition as well as her concerns about her grown children. She is lonely living by herself and nonverbally expressed her desire to have a more united family.

The patient seems to gain her power from the external affirmations of others and may well be very insecure in her single life and that her youngest daughter is now distracted by having to tend to her newborn child.

I felt that Hope related to me as a one-up minister. I think she found solace in knowing that I was clergy, and she felt comfortable and safe speaking to me.

Sociological/Cultural Concerns

Hope trusts the hospital staff and the physicians who are caring for her. She has been here before and received good, friendly, and compassionate care. It might well be that she turns to this form of attention when her family is not readily available for her socially and personally. Relationships are important to her and her Hispanic culture.

This patient will return home to living alone and without as much family contact as she wishes. This may trigger more stress and lead to further "headaches."

Theological Concerns

To this patient, God and her faith are extremely important, as well as having a strong relationship with her family. Her ultimate concern was relief of her physical pain and for the faith and lifestyles of her family. Hope demonstrated her namesake of hope and trust in God, who can deliver healing of her physical ailments as well as spiritual healing in her family. For me, I thought of the physical and personal hardships of Ruth, who persevered the long trials as she relied upon her faith in God to provide.

Personal Meaning

Personally, I was encouraged by her faith and upbeat spirit despite her unspoken loneliness and frustration. While she was not happy with her present situation, she did have a deep faith that would allow her to persevere through the current trial.

Assessment of the Chaplain

I feel that this patient experienced me as a minister who gave her emotional and spiritual stability during a frustrating time. At first impression, I thought that this patient may be magnifying her symptoms somewhat for attention purposes. As I spoke with her, she stopped exhibiting the dramatic moaning and body rubbing within just a few seconds of starting our conversation.

My feelings about this patient were of someone who was primarily mad and lonely, allowing her tension headaches to be exacerbated by her emotional state. I related the biblical parallel of Paul's life of struggles and how he endured his physical pain by his strong faith in God. I feel that I offered Hope understanding and empathy during our session together.

Future Opportunities. What might you do differently if given the chance?

I probably should have delved deeper into her loneliness issues and asked more specific questions about her family concerns.

To the Reader

- What are your initial thoughts about this encounter?
- Do you agree or disagree with how the chaplain functioned?

- Would you have led the conversation differently or explored other areas of concern?
- Did the chaplain function professionally and with empathy and compassion?
- How was the spirituality of the individual assessed?
- Did the chaplain possess good skill sets in some areas and weak ones in others? What were those?
- After reading this verbatim, are you aware of any skill set areas that you may need to improve upon?
- From the psychological perspective, what is the level of emotional awareness/expressivity? What are the major needs or conflicts (expressed and not expressed)? How do you perceive each person's self-image? Where is the power/control in this encounter (internal/external)? Did they relate to the chaplain as one up, one down, or as a peer?
- Were there any sociological and cultural concerns involved with this chaplain-family encounter? If so, what might they have been?
- Did you derive any personal meaning or connection from this verbatim?

VERBATIM 2

Chronic Debilitating Disease

Known Facts. Patient "Juan" was admitted into the hospital by his primary physician two days prior. He is seventy-five years old and is Baptist. I had met Juan and spent about fifteen minutes with him the day before on an initial pastoral visit. From that visit, I learned that his grandfather emigrated here from Spain and founded a small town (near the hospital) where he had sold his roadside produce for many years. Juan is illiterate, and despite a strong family of faith, he has been more of a rebel for much of his life. I had met his sister and brother-in-law the day before, and they also had concern over his health and emotions. His recent health concerns have caused him great pause and self-reflection. Today, as I was with a patient across the hall from his room, I noticed a nurse standing at my door. I motioned for her to come into the room since I was about to leave. She waited until I was finished and stayed outside in the hall. As I stepped out, she asked me if I had time to meet with Juan. She had just left his room, and he was crying. To her, he seemed very sad. I said that I would be pleased to go and spend some time with him.

Pastoral Plan. My general pastoral plan for an initial patient visit is to create an open environment for conversation and spiritual dialogue as the patient allows. For this requested follow-up visit, my pastoral plan would include reestablishing a good rapport and dialogue with the patient as I attempt to uncover the cause of his emotional distress, offer my ministry of presence in a helpful way, and give verbal and spiritual support as appropriate.

Description of the Patient and Setting. Since Juan is in an isolation room, I heed the precautions and put on the appropriate protective garments and mask. It also raises my concern about what I might have been exposed to the day before when we talked and prayed. As I enter, Juan is crying in bed. The TV is off, and the overhead lights are off. Juan looks like a stereotypical Mexican cowboy. He is about five feet nine inches tall with long, full sideburns, a heavy mustache, and a rough complexion. The room is quiet and devoid of any personal items, flowers, or cards. While he has had some family members visit, it does not appear that any are staying for any extended periods of time.

The Visit

C1: Hey, Juan. I'm Chaplain _____. Do you remember meeting me yesterday? (Juan nods.) Your nurse told me that you aren't feeling too well today. What's going on?

P1: The doctors believe that I have ALS.

C2: Is that what they told you? (I walk to the other side of his bed and sit down in a chair. I want to get physically closer to Juan so that he can sense my sincerity and know that I am not feeling rushed or distracted. I also sat down to physically express that I am willing to listen and am ready to have a meaningful private conversation with him.)

P2: No. This doctor will not say what I have. He keeps running tests. But my primary doctor told me my symptoms were ALS. I even went and saw two doctors in Mexico a few months ago who both said I have ALS. Both of my younger brothers have died of ALS. (Juan begins sobbing. I pause for a minute or so.)

C3: Was that difficult to watch your brothers suffer with ALS?

P3: Yes. They both passed away about ten years ago after going down physically for quite a while. (Juan continues to weep and wipe his eyes with a facial tissue I handed him).

C4: And now you might have that same disease. That must be overwhelming for you. (Juan continues to cry. After, a long ten-second pause.)

P4: Could you raise the head of my bed a little? (He motions to the buttons on the outside of the bed rails. After the bed is adjusted, I lean forward and relax my arms on the rail, holding my small Bible). When I was a young boy, I helped my grandfather in the produce fields. My father was a minister. As a young man, I dropped out of high school at age fifteen and began working as a cowboy. I would break the wild horses for fifty dollars and shoe them for seven. People from all around would come to me … I also traveled the world for many years with Halliburton working as an oil rig hand. I've seen the Middle East, North Africa, Europe … There wasn't a man around who I couldn't fight and beat up. (Juan talked about his life for nearly twenty minutes. While I initially thought I needed to redirect him back to his health concerns, I realized that he was reliving his past of being a physical strong man who is now facing a debilitating future.)

C5: Juan, it sounds like you were quite a stud for most of your life. How does that make you feel to know that you're losing your strength and physical abilities?

P5: (Juan tears up again for a few seconds. He clears his throat and continues.) It scares me. I have been slowly losing the feeling and use of my right side for the past few years and have to be in a wheelchair from time to time because my right leg gets weak. (Juan begins sobbing again.) And there's no one at home to take care of me when it gets worse. (Juan continues to wipe his eyes.) I have three grown sons. Two of them live far away. My youngest just got out of jail after ten years. He came around asking me for money last year. I've given him so much money over the years, and he is always unappreciative.

Essential Chaplain Skill Sets

This time, he wanted three hundred bucks. I told him no. Then he got mad and threatened me with a big knife. I told him no again and rolled into my bedroom to get something. I got my pistol out from under my mattress, and when turned I around, I saw him standing in front of me. I told him to leave and never come back. He said, "What are you going to do to me, old man? Shoot me? You can't even point the gun right?" I pointed the gun at his crotch and said that if he didn't leave my house, I was going to shoot him.

C6: Has your son come back?

P6: No. Now I'm going to be in a wheelchair for the rest of my life. (Juan tears up again as he looks at the ceiling and shuts his eyes for a moment.)

C7: Are you feeling helpless?

P7: Yes … I know I won't be able to take care of myself. (Juan pauses again and wipes his eyes.) But I do have faith. While I may not have lived life as good as I should have, I do believe in God.

C8: That is good to hear. Who is Christ to you, Juan?

P8: Christ is my Savior. I went to a Baptist church for a while with one of my wives, and I understood God's love and Christ's sacrifice for me.

C9: That is also really good to hear, Juan. As believers, we can take rest and comfort in knowing that God loves us and cares for us even through the strained relationships and physical struggles of our lives here on earth. The apostle Paul lived with a chronic illness and pain, but he kept his faith to see him through the tough times.

P9: I know. (Juan continues to weep.)

C10: There's a book in the Bible called Jeremiah. There's a passage there that I refer to as "God's phone number." Jeremiah 33:3 (NASB) says, "Call to Me and I will answer you, and I will tell you great and might things which you do not know." Later in Revelation, it says that God cherishes our prayers as sweet incense. That's how much God loves each one of His children. It's amazing to think that the Almighty God of all the universe loves to hear my prayers and your prayers, Juan! He wants us to talk and communicate with Him about everything that's in our hearts. I want you to know that God knows what you are feeling today and that He hears your cries. (Juan continues to softly cry and wipe his eyes.)

P10: Can you pray for me?

C11: Juan, I would be honored to do so. What specifically would you like me to pray with you about?

P11: Just a prayer for me would be good.

C12: Dear Almighty God, you are the Creator of all nature and the author of life. You even created humans as your special project to have relationship with you. Throughout Scripture, it says that if we call out to you, you will hear our cries, Lord. Lord, I know that you understand the hurting that Juan has in his heart today. I pray that you will allow him to sense your presence and that you as the Great Physician and Comforter will make yourself known to him today. Please be with Juan and reassure him that he is right in the palm of your hand, even in these stressful times. I pray that your hand will be upon him. In Christ's name, I pray. Amen. (I pause for a moment, wipe back a few of my own tears, and shake his hand.)

P12: Thank you, Pastor.

(I take off the protective gown, gloves, and mask and quietly leave.)

Interpretation and Evaluation

Assessment of the Person

Q: What kind of person is this?
A: Juan is a man who—after a life of physical strength—is now facing a life of permanent disability and loss of independence.
Q: How did you experience your time together?
A: I thought our time together was meaningful and ordained by God.

Psychological Concerns

Q: What is the level of emotional awareness/expressivity?
A: I assessed that Juan was in grief about his physical loss and probable diagnosis of ALS, which had previously taken the lives of his two brothers. He knows the terrible impact that this disease can have on the human body and that it will be fatal.

Q: What are the major needs or conflicts (expressed and not expressed)?
A: I felt that his major need was just to have a listening friend present to help him sort out his feelings that he was having difficulty expressing.

Q: What is this person's self-image? Where is the power/control in the patient's life (internal/external)?
A: Juan drew much of his power throughout his life internally from his physical strength, athleticism, and abilities. While this may have been overcompensated due to his lack of formal education or his perception of that, he may only now be learning to draw upon his own faith in God for strength and comfort.

Q: Did they relate to you one up, one down, or as a peer?
A: I felt that Juan related to me very openly as his pastor and maybe even as a friend. I also felt that this might have been the first time that Juan has ever expressed and communicated so openly about his frustrations.

Sociological/Cultural Concerns

Socially, Juan does not have much family support. While he seems to be a generally nice man, he probably has lived behind a hard, masculine shell that is common with his generation and culture. This type of rough masculinity probably created barriers with his three sons. In his vulnerability at the hospital, the nursing staff and I felt connected to Juan's openness and fears of living alone with this incurable neuromuscular disease.

Chaplain Keith Evans

Theological Concerns

Q: What are the central life issues for the patient?
A: Juan's mortality and fear of death was the key concept that I thought Juan tried to communicate. God has been a distant reality to him, but God and eternity are now beginning to play a much greater role in his life as he searches for meaning and acceptance of his disease.
Q: Did the patient's situation parallel any biblical characters or themes?
A: I think of King Hezekiah who is given a death notice by God due to his own disobedience and that of the Israelites. But the imminent discipline is lifted as he comes back to God in repentance and is allowed fifteen more years of life. While Juan may not be given his malady due to his own personal sin, he is given a chance to draw closer in relationship and trust/obedience to God through the crisis.

Personal Meaning

Q: What personal meaning did you derive from this visit?
A: My second cousin was about eight years older than me. He was an anesthesiologist in Carrollton for many years and came down with ALS/Lou Gehrig's disease. He died in 2010. While I was not personally close to this cousin, I grew up in the same town and watched his life from a distance. I've read his book, which he typed with one finger, about his faith in God through personal suffering (*Change of Flight Plan* by Paul Lanier, MD). I also related to Juan as I understand how it is to lose one's physical strength and abilities—myself on a limited basis, and watching my own father's health decline with his advanced diabetes. From these events, I understand that a handicapped or disabled individual must discover and form a new personal "identity" after events of life change your course or "flight plan."

Assessment of the Chaplain

I believe that Juan experienced me as genuine, caring, and "in the moment." I do not feel that he felt that I was rushing him through the wave of emotions that would flood over him as he was grieving the loss of his former self.

Q: Why did you decide to record this particular visit?
A: I felt God's presence and compassion in the room with Juan and me.
Q: Who are you in the session, and how is this communicated to the patient?
A: Pastor and compassionate friend.
Q: How did you address the psychological, sociological, and theological concerns?
A: I tried to draw out his feelings and hurts to help me understand where he is at psychologically and emotionally.
Q: Describe your ministry to this patient and the various modalities in which you delivered it.
A: I felt that I used active and reflective listening. I alertly listened to the data of his life and discovered the key values of his life that he was indirectly grieving over.
Q: Can you relate any biblical motifs to the patient's situation or theological stance?
A: King Hezekiah, as previously mentioned.
Q: What were your predominant gifts to the patient?
A: Empathy, listening, and presence were the primary gifts given to Juan. These were followed by pastoral insight and prayer.

Future Opportunities. What might you do differently if given the chance?

I'm not sure at this point. I would have liked to have given him a day or so to reflect upon his illness and then had the opportunity to meet with him again to see how he is progressing with his grief.

To the Reader

- What are your initial thoughts about this encounter?
- Do you agree with or disagree with how the chaplain functioned?
- Would you have led the conversation differently or explored other areas of concern?
- Did the chaplain function professionally and with empathy and compassion?
- How was the spirituality of the individual assessed or not?
- Did the chaplain possess good skill sets in some areas and weak ones in others? What were those?
- After reading this verbatim, are you now aware of any skill set areas that you may need to improve upon?
- From the psychological perspective, what is the level of emotional awareness/expressivity? What are the major needs or conflicts (expressed and not expressed)? How do you perceive each person's self-image? Where is the power/control in this encounter (internal/external)? Did Juan relate to the chaplain as one up, one down, or as a peer?
- Were there any sociological and cultural concerns involved with this chaplain-family encounter? If so, what might they have been?
- Did you derive any personal meaning or connection from this verbatim?

VERBATIM 3

Do I Stay or Do I Go?[135]

Known Facts

Chaplain Cheryl was paged to a stroke alert of an elderly female who is a patient in the emergency department. Two family members are present in the emergency area: the patient's son and daughter-in-law (who is a former employer and critical care nurse). Another son and daughter-in-law arrive later, and Chaplain Cheryl reunited with them in the emergency department's main waiting area.

Description of Patient and Setting

Upon entering the emergency department, Chaplain Cheryl encounters the patient's son, Willie, in the hallway. After introductions, they discuss events leading up to the patient's health crisis. Willie's wife, Ronnie, is in the examination room. Upon entering the examination room, the patient answers questions posed by the staff. She is also offering information to the staff. The ministry for this family takes place in the main emergency department waiting area.

---

[135] This "awkward" verbatim was graciously contributed by Rev. Peter L. Ward, DMin. Dr. Ward is a ACPE supervisory student with Banner Health System and a clinical chaplain at Banner Thunderbird Medical Center in Glendale, Arizona.

Chaplain Keith Evans

The Visit

C1: Hi, my name is Cheryl, I'm a part of the emergency department team. I came to be of support to you. Are you the patient's son?
W1: Yes.
C2: I'm sorry. I didn't get your name.
W2: Willie.
C3: Hi, Willie. Was your mom's health challenge sudden?
W3: Yes and no. She called the house earlier after she returned to her care facility from a Wal-Mart run. She couldn't stop coughing. We went right over to the facility, and it became even more apparent that she was ill—so we called 911. They're going to run tests to see if we're dealing with pneumonia only or a stroke in addition to her lungs being filled with fluid.
C4: Rest assured the staff is going to do everything they can to pinpoint and deal with the issue.
(Willie made no comment. He seemed concerned with what was happening in the examination room with his mom, as was I. The curtain was closed.)
C5: Do you have any family with you, Willie?
W4: Yes, my wife is in there, and my brother and his wife are on their way here.
C6: When they call you upon arrival here, we can go out to meet them if you like.
W5: They will probably just ask at the desk. (We both walk into the examination room, and I meet Willie's wife, Ronnie).
C7: Hi, my name is Cheryl. I'm a member of the ED team. I'm a chaplain, and I wanted to come by and offer some support to you and Willie.
R1: Hi, I'm Ronnie, the daughter-in-law.
C8: I see they're doing all they can for your mother-in-law. What is her first name?
R2: Elsie. Yeah, she has a lot going on right now. I was a nurse here for twenty-two years in ICU and surgery. This building that we are in was not built when I worked here all those years.

Essential Chaplain Skill Sets

(Ronnie tells me in emergency medicine jargon everything the staff is doing. She goes on to describe the hospital buildings prior to recent additions. The staff asks Ronnie questions concerning her mother-in-law's health, and she answers them. My colleague informs me that there was another stoke alert that had not been attended to by a chaplain. Willie overhears this).

W6: Why don't you attend to that patient and family?

C8: Okay, I believe I will. Do you need anything?

W7: No sir, we're fine. (I attend to other announced stroke alert and return to check on Willie and Dorothy thirty minutes later)

C9: Ronnie, did your mother-in-law belong to any faith community?

R3: Yes. She was a Seventh Day Adventist. I'm Catholic, but I attended services with her at her church on several occasions. She used to tease me while we were in church. She would say, "Well, I haven't been struck yet for sitting next to a Catholic!" (I laughed.) But she would not go to mass with me. (The attending ED physician enters and asks Ronnie more medical questions. She answers them and asks a few more questions of him, but as he begins to answer, she cuts him off).

R4: (Speaking to the physician) I'm sorry. I didn't mean to be smart. (Once Ronnie and the attending physician seem to establish an understanding, Ronnie asks the staff and attending physician if they knew several former employees and colleagues of hers. The attending physician and the nurses recognize the names. In fact, the person was still employed with the hospital and was in a high administrative position! Well, off to the MRI. I wait with Ronnie and Willie where she and Willie begin to make telephone calls. I'm quiet during this time, hoping perhaps for an opportunity to ask them if I could say a short prayer before the patient returns. As it turns out, they spend 80 percent of the time while the patient is undergoing tests on their phones. The last five to eight minutes, I simply listen to them. Upon the patient's return to the ED room, more medical questions are asked of Ronnie. Ronnie begins to speak with her mother-in-law and is even asked by the nurse to assist with a simple task of which she is delighted).

R5: (Speaking to the nurses) I think I'm going to go out into the lobby and check on Willie. (I proceed out with Ronnie. Once out in the general waiting area, Willie's brother and sister-in-law are now present and speaking to Willie. No introductions are made to me. Ronnie begins to explain the care her mother-in-law has received to this point, the results of certain tests, and medications she is currently receiving in the ED. Willie listens, comments, and the exchange between the two goes on for ten more minutes while I am standing right beside them. I'm beginning to feel pretty awkward).

C10: You must be either the sister and Elsie's son-in-law—or you must be the other brother and you are Elsie's daughter-in-law.

R6: She, like me, is an in-law! Yes, we're both the in-laws!

C11: I figured that. He looks just like his brother. (No comment, just smiles.)

R7: (Speaking to the other brother's wife) Let's go get something to drink. (They get up and head for the door that leads into the lobby.)

C12: Would you like to go to the cafeteria?

R8: Yes.

C13: Go out that door, take a left, and take the south elevators to the lower level.

R9: Thanks. (A conversation continues between the brothers.)

C14: I'm going to give you all some time to yourselves. I'll check on you and your mom later.

W8: Okay, thanks.

C15: God bless. Goodbye now.

Interpretation and Evaluation

Assessment of Patient or Situation

Patient is having a serious health crisis, but no real answers about a prognosis are available at the time. According to the family, the patient is very independent yet needs some assistance with meds. Elsie seems to be the outspoken matriarch of this family who has the love and respect of her daughter-in-laws. Likewise, this family seems very independent and only asks for support when necessary. Perhaps Ronnie's years as a nurse exposed her to chaplain ministry, and perhaps she and Willie have no urgent need for a spiritual care member of the ED team.

Theological Reflection

Affirm others, and if they are not interested in your ministry to them, keep moving! "If people don't welcome you, shake the dust off your feet when you leave" (Luke 9:5).

Future Opportunities

I followed up that evening with Elsie. The family had already left for the evening. I will get input about a possible follow-up visit.

Assessment of Chaplain

Perhaps I missed key opportunities to see if Ronnie would share more of her feelings if I had showed more appreciation for her knowledge of critical care medicine. The other ED staff showed a measure of appreciation and even the attending physician did despite Ronnie's anxious remark early on. I also missed cues that afforded me the option to possibly leave them much earlier than I did.

To the Reader

- What are your initial thoughts about this encounter?
- Do you agree with or disagree with how the chaplain functioned?
- Would you have led the conversation differently or explored other areas of concern?
- Did the chaplain function professionally and with empathy and compassion?
- How was the spirituality of the individual assessed or not?
- Did the chaplain possess good skill sets in some areas and weak ones in others? What were those?
- After reading this verbatim, are you now aware of any skill set areas that you may need to improve upon?
- From the psychological perspective, what is the level of emotional awareness/expressivity? What are the major needs or conflicts (expressed and not expressed)? How do you perceive each person's self-image to be? Where is the power/control in this encounter (internal/external)? Did they relate to the chaplain as one up, one down, or as a peer?
- Were there any sociological and cultural concerns involved with this chaplain-family encounter? If so, what might they have been?
- Did you derive any personal meaning or connection from this verbatim?

VERBATIM 4
Emergency Room Death

Known Facts.

I was helping with spirituality group session with a peer chaplain when I was paged to arrange for a priest to give the sacrament of the sick to an ER patient who had just arrived. By the time I went downstairs, the ER had called the pastoral care office to request a priest for the same patient. By the time I located the priest, who was on another floor visiting patients, the ER contacted pastoral care for the third time. I was able to tell them the priest was on his way down and that I would meet him there with the patient and family as quickly as possible.

Pastoral Plan. My general pastoral plan for an on-call/duty page is to make initial contact with staff, quickly glean whatever pertinent information I can about the patient, and then make my presence and services available.

Description of the Patient and Setting. As I entered the ER, the RN asked if the priest was coming. I affirmed that he was on his way down. The RN stated that they would wait for him and escort him to the bedside just as soon as he arrived. The RN stated that the patient was extremely critical and could pass away at any moment. I went to the three-bed ER room; the patient was in the middle bed with curtains drawn on all sides. I saw a frail Hispanic woman who was probably around seventy years old. She was intubated and also had all the other normal IV and EKG leads that are common with acute ER cases. I also observed that she was still lying on the paramedics' backboard. Two other women were hugging one another. I learn from the RN that they were the patient's daughter and granddaughter.

The Visit

C1: (Softly and speaking slowly.) Hi. (The two women turn and look. They are both weeping and wiping their eyes with tissues).

C2: I'm a chaplain here at the hospital. (Pointing to my name badge) What has happened to your mom?

PD1: She collapsed at home after breakfast. She just slumped over in her chair. (They both begin crying again. I sense their deep pain and heavy anxiety about how this will eventually turn out.)

C3: I'm so sorry. I know you requested a priest to come to perform the sacrament of the sick for your mom. Is that right? (They nod.) Father Anthony is upstairs. He is on his way down now. (The daughter shakes her head in gratefulness.)

PD2: Can he wait until my brother gets here? He is on his way.

C4: I'm not sure if that's best for your mom. The RN says that your mother is very critical, and I want her to receive her sacrament as quickly as possible. (She nods as though she understands the gravity of the matter. The RN greets Father Anthony. Father Anthony quickly walks past the two ladies and positions himself near the patient's head. He anoints her head and hands and performs the sacrament of the sick. I walk to the opposite side of the bed, uncover her other arm, and raise her hand for Father to anoint. Father finishes, gives me a quick blessing of thanks, and leaves without much of any conversation to the family. I think, *All priest—no pastor!* As I stay on the opposite side of the bed, the daughter

Essential Chaplain Skill Sets

and granddaughter step back up to the bed for a few quiet moments.

C5: I know the priest has anointed your mom, but if there is anything meaningful that I do for you, a prayer or another type of ministry, I want to be here for you.

PD3: I can't pray to [*expletive omitted*] God! Why is God doing this? (Wow! That was extremely offensive to me and very unsettling. I felt that shake my core being. I realize that she's frustrated and scared, but that's over the top for me and my faith position. Has this woman's common and vulgar language allowed her to become insensitive to what that word truly means?

The cursing daughter leans over and lays her head on her mother's chest as the granddaughter comforts her. I feel at a loss of words at this moment in her pain. After I regain my composure, I decide not to leave the room. I attempt to continue ministering to them. Can I salvage this patient encounter and make it a positive chaplain experience for them? Can I initiate some form of dialogue where ministry can be spurred?)

C6: I don't know. We don't know why this has happened to your mom today. (At this moment, a very large, intimidating, bald Hispanic man comes in. He's about five foot nine and is probably pushing three hundred lbs. I notice that he has vulgar tattoos all over both arms, and his head even has tattoos of ram's horns on both sides. I think, *Oh great! If it's not going well with the daughter, I wonder how it will go with this guy.* First impressions tell me that he wants to be known as a tough-as-nails type of guy. This may get interesting.)

PGD1: Uncle Frankie! (As they quickly hug, I see that he is visibly shaken to see his mother in her current state. His eyes are teary.)

F1: How bad is she?

PGD2: They say she had a massive heart attack and that she may not make it. (As the granddaughter says this, the ER doctor and attending RN come in and line up on my side of the bedside. I think that this staging makes it look like it's us against them.)

D1: I'm Dr. Santos. Your mom's heart had a lot of damage with her heart attack, and she is dying. We have tried all that we can do. We have maxed out all the medicine that we can give her, and her body is not responding. I don't believe that she'll be with us much longer. (The family is wide-eyed. I notice a rage like the Incredible Hulk welling up in Frank. He raises both arms and slams them down on the bedrails. He begins a screaming, cursing rant and aggressively blames the doctor, the nurse, and me! *What did I do? I just got here too!*)

D2: Security! Sir, the hospital will not have that behavior here. We have tried all that we can do for your mom! (The doctor quickly leaves the RN and me standing there. The RN tries to calm Frank down in the midst of his ongoing bellowing. He slams his hands down on the bed, shaking it—and his mom—on the bed. I notice three security officers arrive. The RN finally leaves, leaving me alone. Now it really feels like me against them. Frank begins to weep crocodile tears.)

C7: Hey, Frank. (He looks over at me.) I'm the hospital chaplain. I'm sorry about your mom. (He stares at me for what seems like a very long and awkward five seconds and then reenters his body from his out-of-body experience and emotional rage.)

F2: Thank you. (Over the next ten minutes or so, most of the family and I are quiet. The security officers begin to give the family more space and back off into the main ER hallway. Frank goes through waves of heavy emotion and repeatedly lays over his mother's torso and pets her hands and kisses her face. The RN comes in and checks her pulse, listens to her heart, and indicates that the patient has died. The emotions of both kids swell back up in heavy sadness and grief. Frank continues weeping. "Momma, Momma, what am I going to do without you, Momma?" He picks up her head and shoulders and hugs her. I'm getting scared that he's going to damage her body—and fluids are about to go squirting everywhere!

Essential Chaplain Skill Sets

Frank gently sets her head and torso back down on the bed. A small-framed Hispanic gentleman enters the room with two others. I learn that he's the patient's brother. He looks at her and collapses. I run to the nurses' desk and get help. They get him seated, question him, and offer care. They discover that he is a diabetic who hadn't eaten much that morning. He drinks some juice and recovers in a few minutes.

PD4: She's in God's hands now, Frankie. She's going to be okay. We know where she is.

(That's a quick change of mind-set from the God-cursing daughter. She's beginning to comfort and minister to her brother, which is rather confusing behavior.)

F3: Momma! What am I going to do without you? You're my life, Momma! (Frank looks at his sister and talks like a helpless child.)

F4: What are we going to do with Momma gone? What are we going to do?

PD5: We're going to make it, Frankie. (The daughter and granddaughter begin to call other family members. Frank continues to weep, and I sense that it's the right time to step in as a minister for him.)

C8: Frank, would it be okay if I pray with you? (Frank keeps his head down and never looks up.

He simply reaches out his huge hand toward me like a little child wanting to be held. *Wow. God just opened up and handed me this opportunity to minister to Frankie.* I grab his enormous outstretched hand with one hand and lay my other hand over the back of his huge, burly neck and head.)

C9: Dear Almighty God, we ask for your great grace and mercy upon Ms. Garza as we commit her spirit to you. Her earthly body suffers no more. May your comfort and grace also be upon Frankie and her family right now. Allow this family to share their emotions and grieve in whatever way is needed. Please, Lord, let them know that you are the great Comforter and to feel your presence in this place despite their heaviness and sadness. And please give them the strength to continue on without Ms. Garza, to allow them to become the son, the daughter, and grandchildren that she would be so proud of. Please give them that strength, God. We pray this in the name of the Father, the Son, and the Holy Spirit. Amen. (Frank looks up and squeezes my hand very tightly.)

F5: Thank you.

C10: You are very welcome, Frank, and my condolences to all of the family here in the loss of Ms. Garza.

C11: Everyone may stay here with her as long as you wish. (I remain for another five minutes or so and then make some parting words. I let them know that if they need me, the RN can page me. I make my exit and nod to the security team and ER nurses' station (for some reason, they are all looking my way). Even though I don't believe I did very much ministry work, remaining in the tension with the family emotionally drained me. I'm glad it's essentially over—and the emotions have calmed.)

Interpretation and Evaluation

Assessment of the Person

My assessment is that the deceased was very maternal and nurturing to her son and daughter. While she may have had chronic illness, the suddenness of her death took the family by surprise. I initially assessed Frank as an aggressive and violent man, but he later melted into a three-hundred-pound teddy bear who needed outside comfort and help. The daughter and other family members remained polite and respectful yet distant to me as clergy.

Psychological Concerns

It was apparent to me that Frank wanted to be seen as very self-assured and worked off his own inner power. I did not sense that he had any overt mental or psychological deficits.

Essential Chaplain Skill Sets

Sociological/Cultural Concerns

The family dynamics within this Hispanic culture was familiar to me since I have experienced the mother-son bond to be extremely embedded with other Hispanics in many other patient encounters. As I did not hear any mention of a spouse to the deceased—or a father's presence to the grown kids—I can only assume that the son-daughter bond will continue and strengthen as they are now faced with leading their families.

Theological Concerns

To this patient's family, God may be only a transcendent deity to them. This was displayed by their need of priestly rituals and the need *to do* the proper thing for Ms. Garza before her death. I did not see that the family experienced God with any personal-ness in their lives until my prayer experience with Frankie. For a theological integration/reflection for this situation, the closest biblical account may be that of the Gadarene demoniac (Mark 5). He was possibly trapped by his own demons and was in desperate need of outside help.

Personal Meaning

Personally, my heart was very sad for this family in their sudden loss. As a chaplain, I initially felt dismissed or simply unrecognized in the midst of the early and intense emotions. I understand why that occurred and do not feel that it was personal in any way. Personally, God has met me at times of my own intense frustrations. He has calmed me down and given me great peace, comfort, and strength in knowing that He cares.

Assessment of the Chaplain

This encounter was my first experience with an emotionally raging family member following a death. I was not sure how much to allow with Frank's physical hugging, lifting, and almost lying on top of his petite, deceased mother. I did not want to stop the grief by interfering, but I was concerned about her body. I felt that I stayed calm in the midst of a highly tense, emotional storm, which hopefully allowed Frank and his family to process their emotions more effectively and productively. Even though I may have missed other pastoral care conversations in this encounter, I felt that I did hold on to the ministry role well enough, allowing the ER staff to focus their attention on what they do best.

Future opportunities. What might you do differently if given the chance?

I may have elected to dismiss myself too early. By remaining, I'm sure further pastoral care conversations over grief and bereavement issues could have been fostered with this family. Or is there a better time for that after the critical incident has taken place?

To the Reader

- What are your initial thoughts about this encounter?
- Do you agree with or disagree with how the chaplain functioned?
- Would you have led the conversation differently or explored other areas of concern?
- Did the chaplain function professionally and with empathy and compassion?
- How was the spirituality of the individual assessed or not?
- Did the chaplain possess good skill sets in some areas and weak ones in others? What were those?
- After reading this verbatim, are you now aware of any skill set areas that you may need to improve upon?
- From the psychological perspective, what is the level of emotional awareness/expressivity? What are the major needs or conflicts (expressed and not expressed)? How do you perceive each person's self-image to be? Where is the power/

control in this encounter (internal/external)? Did they relate to the chaplain as one up, one down, or as a peer?
- Were there any sociological and cultural concerns involved with this chaplain-family encounter? If so, what might they have been?
- Did you derive any personal meaning or connection from this verbatim?

VERBATIM 5

A Behavioral Unit Encounter

Known Facts

Patient "Ken" was admitted into the hospital's behavioral unit a few days before. At this particular hospital setting, the chaplains have the privilege and opportunity to lead spirituality group sessions twice a week. Another chaplain and I had just completed the spirituality group, and everyone had left the room. I was completing the needed paperwork concerning who attended and their level of interaction and social functioning. Ken walked back into the room and wished to talk privately.

Pastoral Plan

My pastoral plan for any random initial visit is to create an open environment for conversation and spiritual dialogue as the patient allows, as prompted by my questions on their spirituality and their current concerns. With this case of a spirituality group, my goal is to give a short devotional/teaching moment that may connect to their story and then facilitate an intentional conversation about the topic as it relates to their lives and behaviors.

Essential Chaplain Skill Sets

Description of the Patient and Setting

Ken was a thin thirty-year-old Caucasian male and was about six foot tall. He had a short haircut and no visible tattoos or body piercings. He was alert, conversational, and oriented to time, place, and surroundings. He was appropriately dressed. From his previous interaction in the spiritual group setting, I did not observe that Ken exhibited any gross behavioral dysfunctions or other possible organic cognitive issues as he revealed appropriate social interaction and comprehension skills. I was standing completing the paperwork at a countertop as he entered the room to my left.

The Visit

P1: Chaplain, could I ask you something? (I looked up to see Ken moving slowly into the room. I assume that he does not want to disturb me but wants more to talk to me.)

C1: Yea, Ken. What's on your mind?

P2: I would like to ask you a question. I've been in four detox units and six rehab facilities over the past ten years. I'm thirty years old. I'm a mechanic, and I used to drink with my buddies too much. I'd go on benders and then try to get sober. I was raised in church. My dad is a retired military, so we moved a lot when I was younger. We moved here when I was a teenager. That's when I started smoking weed and drinking. After high school, I moved to Ohio to work as a welder and got my girlfriend pregnant. We got married when my little boy was two months old. I lost my job, so we moved back here.

C2: (We are both leaning up against the counter and facing each other. I am nodding to show that I am understanding what he is saying, but I am also aware that Ken may actually have a lot on his mind. I'm also beginning to wonder where this conversation is going and what question he wants to ask me.)

P3: My dad is a deacon and Sunday school teacher. I was raised Baptist and went to church here with my wife and kids. I've

Chaplain Keith Evans

got three now. My oldest boy is seven. I never seem to have problems getting a job, but it is keeping the jobs that are a problem for me. I start off good, but then I eventually start drinking with the other guys from work, and I get myself in trouble.

C3: (I nod and quietly say, "Uh-huh." I want to let him know that I'm still tracking his story, however long it may become.)

P4: I went on a bender one time, picked up a case, and went to jail. (I'm not sure what he meant by that, but I stayed quiet, not wanting to interrupt his thoughts.) While I was in jail, I began wanting to get a dragon tattoo, so I called my dad to help me find a good drawing of one. But when you're incarcerated, anything anyone sends you—like a book—must come directly from the store. So my dad ordered a bunch of books from Borders—anything that has to do with dragons—and sent them to me. One of the books I liked the most had this great picture of a dragon, but it was about Buddhism and meditation. So here's my question. I want to know what you think.

C4: (Finally! The question. I stay mentally engaged and lean forward slightly.)

P5: During the group session, the psalms that we read from triggered my question. (I had used Psalm 40 as my teaching moment. It is David's praise of waiting patiently in the pit and mire of a dreadful situation, while not giving in to false wisdom and impatience. In verse 4, it said not to worship any false idols. Ken pointed to this verse as he asked his question.) Is it okay to read *My Utmost for His Highest* devotionals, my Bible, and read and meditate from the Buddhist writings? My wife doesn't care as long as it helps me. Do you think that it's okay for me to read that?

C5: Well, you said that you are a Baptist who was raised in the Christian faith. What does reading the Buddhist meditations do for you?

P7: The readings are more of just relaxing my mind. I'm not praying to Buddha. Do you think that is bad?

Essential Chaplain Skill Sets

C6: No. I think that it is good to develop the spiritual disciplines like prayer, meditations, and reading. To me, the difference would be who you are praying to and meditating toward. As a Christian, my focus would be toward my Creator and Savior. I used to read Oswald Chambers quite a bit after I was "in my pit" a few years ago. His writings were very beneficial for my spiritual growth. When you meditate, are you looking for answers within yourself or from above?

P7: From God. I also do yoga but just to stretch.

C7: Yoga stretches are fine. The Eastern transcendental meditation would not be considered Christian. (I'm aware that I'm probably giving him too much information. I need to engage him more in a reflective way.) What have you been doing about controlling your drinking and binges when the urges and cravings come on?

P8: I have a sponsor. He holds an AA meeting at my church that I attend. He doesn't live far from me. I feel bad calling him late at night, but he says that it is okay.

C8: Since he is your sponsor, I'm sure he is fine with it. But what else helps?

P9: My medication. When I get off it, I start to stress more and begin drinking. I keep telling myself that one drink won't hurt. I want to be there for my wife and boys. I'm so tired of this back-and-forth stuff.

C9: It's pretty frustrating for you?

P10: Yeah. Hopefully this time, I can really make it stick. I get out of here in a few days. (The conversation lingers.) Would you pray for me?

C10: I'd be happy to pray for you and your family, Ken. (I place my hand on his upper back, and he places his hand on my shoulder.) Dear most gracious heavenly Father. You are the all-knowing and all-powerful God of all Creation. You know what Ken has been struggling with all these years. I pray that you keep giving him strength for each day to resist those incredible urges and cravings he steadily fights. Continue to give him a hunger and thirst for righteousness as he reads, meditates, and studies your Word. I pray that he can become the godly man, the father, and the husband that you so desire for him to become. Give him the ability to rely upon you more and more and to be a great witness of your grace and mercy in his life. Remind him of his blessings each and every day, and I pray that one day, his name will be a great legacy, like David who was a man after God's heart. I humbly pray this in the blessed name of our Savior. Amen. (After the prayer, Ken gives me a big hug and walks out with his head down. He stops at the door, and I notice that he is crying.)

P11: Wow ... I've got to dry this up.

C11: (I smile and wink. Ken smiles back at me, wipes his eyes, and jokingly cranes his neck forward. He quickly looks both ways down the hall, stands up straight, and walks out of the room. I stand there smiling and look at the door, enjoying the past moment of ministry and thanking God for using me in Ken's life today. I think, *I wonder if he ever got that dragon tattoo?* I shake my head and resume my small pile of paperwork.)

Interpretation and Evaluation

Assessment of the Person

- What are your initial thoughts about this encounter?
- Do you agree with or disagree with how the chaplain functioned?
- Would you have led the conversation differently or explored other areas of concern?
- Did the chaplain function professionally and with empathy and compassion?
- How was the spirituality of the individual assessed or not?
- Did the chaplain possess good skill sets in some areas and weak ones in others? What were those?

- After reading this verbatim, are you now aware of any skill set areas that you may need to improve upon?
- From the psychological perspective, what is the level of emotional awareness/expressivity? What are the major needs or conflicts (expressed and not expressed)? How do you perceive each person's self-image to be? Where is the power/control in this encounter (internal/external)? Did they relate to the chaplain as one up, one down, or as a peer?
- Were there any sociological and cultural concerns involved with this chaplain-family encounter? If so, what might they have been?
- Did you derive any personal meaning or connection from this verbatim?

Sociological/Cultural Concerns

- How does the patient relate himself/herself to the hospital environment?
- How does the nursing and medical staff then relate back to this patient?
- Is there a supporting community surrounding this patient?
- What sort of environment will this patient be returning to?
- What is your awareness of the patient's cultural or ethnic context?

Theological Concerns

- What are the central life issues for the patient?
- What is the patient's ultimate concern?
- What is the key concept this patient attempted to communicate to you?
- Who is God to this patient?
- How does this patient experience God?

- Did you witness/experience any understanding of grace, providence, repentance, forgiveness, resurrection, reverence, hope, fellowship, etc. in the patient's life?
- If the patient were to preach a sermon, what might it be like?
- What is the meaning and significance of life (and illness) for this patient?
- Did the patient's situation parallel any biblical characters or themes?

Personal Meaning

- What personal meaning did you derive from this visit?
- What connections did you make to your own faith/personal journey that informed your visit?

Assessment of the Chaplain

- How do you imagine this patient experienced you?
- What sort of emotional impact did this patient have on you?
- What were your feelings toward the patient in the session?
- Did the patient change over your time together? If so, how?
- How did you make yourself available to be used pastorally or for growth?
- Who are you in the session, and how is this communicated to the patient?
- How did you address the psychological, sociological, and theological concerns?
- Describe your ministry to this patient and the various modalities in which you delivered it.
- Can you relate any biblical motifs to the patient's situation or his or her theological stance?
- What were your predominant gifts to the patient (hope, empathy, teaching, self-disclosure, humor, love, insight, understanding, etc.)?

Future Opportunities. What might you do differently if given the chance?

- How might this patient benefit from your continued ministry?
- Did you learn things in the interview that would cause you to reset your pastoral goals?
- What might some ongoing areas of development be for you and the patient as a result of this visit?

VERBATIM 6

Brain Mass

Known Facts

Per the daily floor census at hospital, I know that "Jessica" is a thirty-six-year-old Christian. Since this was an initial visit, no information on her diagnosis or reason for her admit was available to me.

Pastoral Plan

My general pastoral plan for the initial patient visit is to introduce myself as part of the health-care team that is available and to create an open environment for conversation and spiritual dialogue as the patient allows.

Description of the Patient and Setting

As I enter her single room, Jessica is sitting on her bed in a sweat top, pants, and shoes. It appears that she was about to be discharged. There are five other women in the room. A birthday cake, balloons, and a few small gifts are on her tray table. I smile and introduce myself to Jessica and the women. I claim my chaplain presence and lean up against the wall near the bathroom door beside her bed to allow a relaxed presence toward all in the room. As I pause, the women say goodbye to Jessica, give her hugs, and leave the room.

Jessica looks at me and says that the ladies are her sisters. As I look at all of their culturally diverse faces, I assume that Jessica is either a foster sibling or part of a local women's shelter or ministry. The last lady (of Filipino descent) hugs Jessica. They share a prolonged firm hold of each other. Jessica begins tearing up and crying. She says, "You all are nicer to me than my own family has ever been. Thank you for coming and celebrating my birthday today." As her last friend leaves the room, I keep looking at Jessica. She catches my eye for a few brief silent seconds and then softly says, "Oh, Chaplain." She slumps down and places her head in her hands. It is obvious that there's much more going on than meets the eye.

The Visit

C1: Hey, Jessica. I'm the main chaplain for the floor. I just wanted to stop by and meet you today. Is today your birthday? (She regains her composure, raises her head, sits up straight, and wipes her eyes.)

P1: Yes. My friends brought me a cake and a gift. They have been nicer to me than my own messed-up family.

C2: It's nice that you have such good friends. Have you all gone through similar things in life?

P2: Yes … they are my new family. We've all struggled in life, and we all help out with a new recovery center.

C3: Yeah. You said they were your sisters, but I didn't think each of you came from the same set of parents. (We exchange smiles. We both understood that what I said was extremely obvious.)

C4: It sounds like you're doing well for yourself now. Has it not always been that way? (Jessica immediately begins crying. I walk over to a chair that is facing the end of her bed and sit down. I want to let her know that I want to hear her story and that I'm not rushed.)

P3: I'm scared. I don't know why God is allowing this to happen! I've changed my ways. I've stopped using drugs. I've given up men. I've stopped smoking. Things were looking good. I've been going to Community Bible Church. I'm trying to have "good fruit" in my life. I have a whole new set of great friends, and I have been helping out in a new rehab facility. (Tears stream down both her cheeks, and her eyes are very red and puffy. She repeatedly wipes her face with her sleeve.)

P4: One of my doctors came in last night and told me I have a brain tumor. As she said it, she put her hand to her mouth as though she didn't want to tell me! I asked what she meant, and she wouldn't tell me any more. She just said that Dr. Wilson would have to tell me more. I don't understand what she meant. (I try to put this information together quickly in my mind, but there is probably much more to this story that I don't know about yet ... I decide to remain quiet and give her my fully undivided attention and let her know that I'm listening and hearing her. I nod a few times and make sure that my body language is telling her that I'm tracking her story and that I'm following closely.)

P5: They say that I may lose my right eye and may go fully blind. What if they can't stop the tumor? I don't want to die! I've asked God to forgive me for my past sins, and I know that He has. I've been waiting thirty-six years to get things going well, and now I'm about to.

(She starts crying again and wiping her eyes.)

C4: I'm sorry, Jessica, that this is happening. It sounds as if you are now ready to really live.

(She very intently looks at me through her tears and nods. A knock is heard, and the door slowly opens. A petite, trim doctor pauses when she notices that I'm not a friend or family. I motion for her to enter. She looks at Jessica and then back at me.)

C5: Hi, Doc. You're not interrupting. I think you've come just at the right time. Jessica is really needing some answers right now. (I read the name of the physician's lab coat: Dr. Wilson, infectious disease specialist. I wonder what Jessica's full diagnosis is. If this is an infectious disease physician, why aren't any contact or other precautions listed on the door?)

D1: What's happening, Jess? (From the casualness and tone of Dr. Wilson's conversation with Jessica, I presume that they have a long history together. Dr. Wilson sits down beside me, leans forward, and gives Jessica her full attention. For the next five to ten minutes, Jessica repeats much of what she just told me—and she begins crying again.)

D2: Jess, get a hold of yourself. You're beginning to spiral! We still need to find out what is going on with the brain mass.

P6: I'm thirty-six years old, and I don't want to die! (Jessica looks intently at Dr. Wilson. I'm comfortable with being a fly on the wall since Jessica needs good, solid information from a physician she trusts to overcome her fears and this emotional crisis.)

P7: I'm scared, Dr. Wilson. They said I could lose my eye.

D3: Who told you that?

P8: The therapist.

D4: No, you aren't going to lose your eye. If we don't treat it aggressively right now, you may lose more vision in your right eye, and it could even spread to your other eye. But you're not going to lose your eye. I looked at the images and spoke with the radiologist. They feel that it may just be an old scar and not even a histo cyst, Jess. It's only a small spot on your brain, and we will treat it. You're going to be okay. (Jessica seems to begin calming down from being reassured by the good information given to her from someone she trusts.)

D6: All of your other tests we ran look good. There are no lab indicators for any histo cysts, and your HIV has been under control for the past six months. You've gained weight and look good. (Now there's the bigger picture of her past health condition that helps me put this situation into a better context for a pastoral conversation. They speak back and forth for another fifteen minutes. Dr. Wilson is doing a good job getting Jessica to focus on facts and not just her momentary feelings. I'm halfway expecting that Dr. Wilson is about to tell her to suck up those tears and put on her big-girl panties!)

P9: I know I've been improving. I've been working hard to get my health and my life back. I've waited thirty-six years for this, and I don't want to lose it. (I hear Jessica expressing intense anticipatory grief for possibly losing her dreams and future aspirations. I also feel that she may truly want meaning and purpose in her life.)

C6: Jessica, if you're ready to really live now—then you will. I believe that you have already begun to do so. (They both look at me as if to convey that they are glad I said that.)

D4: Tell you what, Jess, I'm going to go out now and order some more tests. Get ready. It's going to be a bunch of blood draws. How are your veins doing? (She rolls up her sleeves and reveals her bruised forearms to Dr. Wilson.)

P9: The right side has been more difficult for the nurses.

D5: Okay. We'll do our best on the left. Hang in there, Jess. I'll be right back. (Dr. Wilson leaves the room, and we sit quietly for a few seconds. I want to reframe what I heard and understand what is going on for Jessica to allow her to process everything better.)

C7: It sounds like you've had a long haul with your health problems.

P10: Yes, it has been. And just when I thought things were going good.

C8: But it seems that Dr. Wilson is definitely on top of everything that is going on. Don't you believe so?

P11: She is. I trust her.

C9: I also see that God has been right here with you during this storm. Dr. Wilson showed up just at the right time, didn't she? (Jessica finally smiles. The fixer in me quietly screams, "All right. It's about time!")

P12: Yes, she did.

C10: Jessica, this may sound a little cheesy, but I heard someone say one time that in the storms in our lives—when we are getting royally soaked with problems—God still can teach us to dance in the rain. Does that make sense to you? (She nods. I sense that Jessica and I are emotionally tired and that I may

Essential Chaplain Skill Sets

need to wrap up this encounter. I stand up and walk over to her bedside.)

C11: You said earlier that you want so much to have good fruit in your life. I think it's beginning to happen. It just takes time to really fertilize your spiritual soil and nurture your roots. Be patient with yourself—and let God work at His pace. I would like to pray with you and then just give you time to think about everything. Would that be okay?

P13: That would be great, Chaplain. (Jessica is sitting crossed-legged on her bed. I step closer, place my right hand on her upper back near her neck, and notice that she has her hands on her knees. She turns her palms up toward heaven, and we exchange a quick glance with each other and then bow our heads.)

C12: Dear most gracious God. We bow our heads before you in reverence and honor knowing that You are our Creator, Sustainer, and Redeemer Lord. We recognize that You already know what Jessica has been going through with her health. You know that she so desires to live a better life. I ask for your hand of grace and mercy to be upon her today. Please give her doctors and nursing team the wisdom and discernment of how to best treat her problems. I also pray that You will make yourself known to her. Allow her to feel your presence with her in this room in a real and new way. Continue being her Great Physician and Comforter, Lord. We pray this in Christ's name. Amen. (We both wipe a few tears from our eyes.) Jessica, would you mind if I stop by tomorrow to see how you're doing?

P14: That would great if you can. Thank you, Chaplain.

C13: Happy birthday, Jessica.

Chaplain Keith Evans

Interpretation and Evaluation

Assessment of the Person

Jessica was very open and expressive—even to a complete stranger. She appeared self-confident and assured of herself when we first met. We connected quickly as she emotionally reached out revealing her vulnerability.

Psychological Concerns

It was apparent to me that Jessica was in an emotional crisis due to poor and incomplete information from some previous lab/imaging tests. As Dr. Wilson stated, she was emotionally spiraling. She regained her emotions, and the crisis stabilized once a proper interpretation of the situation was given to her. I felt that Jessica related to me as a one-up minister. I think she found solace in knowing I was a minister and that she felt comfortable and safe speaking to me.

Sociological/Cultural Concerns

Jessica deeply trusts her primary doctor, Dr. Wilson. I feel that developing strong, healthy relationships are very important to her at this time in her life—and that she may not have had these for many years. I did not discover whether or not she had any children or family nearby. It appeared that her five "sisters" were her only family and gave her much emotional and spiritual support.

Theological Concerns

I gathered that, God and her faith have become very important to this patient. She also deeply desires to become useful in helping others overcome their struggles of life or "good fruit" as she put it. This closely parallels the biblical parables of the four soils and the branch and the vine in John 4 and 15.

Personal Meaning

Personally, I was touched by her deep desire to be used by God in a meaningful way in another person's life. Her past life of selfishness and self-destruction was held in stark contrast to her new desires. The news that that may not occur crushed her emotionally and spiritually. I have had similar lapses with frustration. I was encouraged by her faith and how God is working in her life.

Assessment of the Chaplain

I feel that this patient experienced me as a minister who gave her emotional and spiritual stability during a frustrating time.

Future Opportunities. What might you do differently if given the chance?

I would probably cut off the pastoral conversation portion of our encounter a bit earlier due to the time and energy she expended with Dr. Wilson. I would have liked to have delved deeper into identifying how she is dealing with her HIV and other health consequences from her former drug use. When I attempted to return, she had been dismissed.

To the Reader

- What are your initial thoughts about this encounter?
- Do you agree with or disagree with how the chaplain functioned?
- Would you have led the conversation differently or explored other areas of concern?
- Did the chaplain function professionally and with empathy and compassion?
- How was the spirituality of the individual assessed or not?
- Did the chaplain possess good skill sets in some areas and weak ones in others? What were those?

- After reading this verbatim, are you now aware of any skill set areas that you may need to improve upon?
- From the psychological perspective, what is the level of emotional awareness/expressivity? What are the major needs or conflicts (expressed and not expressed)? How do you perceive each person's self-image to be? Where is the power/control in this encounter (internal/external)? Did they relate to the chaplain as one-up, one-down, or as a peer?
- Were there any sociological and cultural concerns involved with this chaplain-family encounter? If so, what might they have been?
- Did you derive any personal meaning or connection from this verbatim?

VERBATIM 7

Hallucinations or Spiritual?

Known Facts

Per the daily floor census at the medical center, I know that "Wallace" is a forty-eight-year-old Pentecostal. Since this was an initial visit, no information on his diagnosis or reason for his admittance was available to me.

Pastoral Plan

My general pastoral plan for the initial patient visit is to introduce myself as part of the health-care team that is available and to create an open environment for conversation and spiritual dialogue as the patient allows.

Description of the Patient and Setting

As I enter the room, Wallace is in a single room. He is a large white man on a wound-management air mattress. All the lights are on, and the blinds are pulled up to let full sunlight into the room. A laptop computer is set up on his bed tray. Religious books and materials are also on the tray. His sheets cover his legs, and he was wearing a hospital gown. He is unshaven, and his stringy, disheveled hair partially covers one eye.

Chaplain Keith Evans

The Visit

C1: Good afternoon. I'm _____, a chaplain in the hospital. (He nods in acknowledgment and smiles as I approach.) I'm the chaplain for this floor, and I try to stop by and meet everyone who comes to the hospital. I like to let everyone know that I am part of the health-care team for you.

P1: It's nice to meet you. (Is this a frequent flyer? What's his story and long-term illness? He looks tired and washed out as I look at him more intently.)

C2: It sounds like being ill isn't anything new to you?

P2: No. I'm tired. (He does look ill. And how tall is this guy? He is sitting up in bed, and his legs are nearly touching the footboards.)

C3: What have you been suffering with?

P3: I hear Satan's voice. (Okay, I wasn't expecting that from him, but he does have a certain look about him. He's pretty strung-out looking. Is he mentally tracking well? I don't want to dismiss him. I want to keep him engaged in good pastoral conversation.)

C4: Oh, what does the voice sound like?

P4: He sounds like mine—just not as hoarse as mine is today.

C5: How long has Satan been talking to you?

P6: Since 2001.

C6: That's a long time, Wallace. Doesn't it make you pretty tired to hear the voices for so long?

P6: Yes.

C7: What do you do to help you not hear his voice?

P7: Pray. I also read the Bible a lot. I think Satan is mad at me for my faith and my witness for God. I am like Job. I have boils all over my body, which is why I've been in the hospital so much. (Wallace pulls the sheets off his legs, and there are huge seeping sores all over both legs. I see some sores on his forearms. Maybe he is telling the truth. He definitely has a

Essential Chaplain Skill Sets

point about feeling like Job. I raise my hands off the bed rails and shift my weight back a few inches.)

C8: Wallace, you *do* have reason to think you're a present-day Job.

P8: Yes. Satan is constantly attacking me, but God protects me. Satan is attacking everywhere. Did you know if you go to certain websites, they'll hack into Christian sites like Pat Robertson's, Billy Graham's, and others? (I smile and nod to show that I'm listening.) Satan has even told me who the Antichrist is.

C9: Really? Who is that?

P9: He's European. He has a Jewish name, but he's a European Gentile. He's Count Rothschild, a wealthy financier.

C10: Really? I haven't heard of him. (I'm not an end-of-times conspiracy theorist, and I try to stay engaged with Wallace to discover another ministry angle, if possible, that we can uncover and process together.)

C11: When do you hear the voices?

P10: The voices come at different times throughout the day. I'm not scared by them anymore. I just listen now and start praying to God to overcome the evil attacks. Most people think I'm crazy when I start telling them this stuff.

C11: I do believe what you're saying, Wallace. I've had other patients before who have had auditory hallucinations. I don't think that all hallucinations are fully organic in nature. I think many can be spiritual in nature as well. I don't believe that everyone who hears something is trippin'.

P11: Thanks. My doctor is making me have a psychiatric evaluation today. [Note: This patient encounter lasted about twenty-five minutes in its entirety, and not all of the conversation is recorded in this verbatim.]

C12: So, what else can I do for you as your chaplain, Wallace?

P12: I wouldn't mind an extra prayer—if that's okay?

C12: Oh, that would be fine with me to pray with you and for you, Wallace. (I place my right hand on his left shoulder, and we bow our heads). Dear most gracious Lord. We bow our heads before you in reverence and honor knowing that You are our Creator, Sustainer, and Redeemer God. You are the great Jehovah Jireh and Jehovah Rapha, the one who provides and gives healing. I ask for your hand of grace and mercy to be upon Wallace today. Please give his doctors and nursing team the wisdom and discernment of how to best treat the lesions on his body. Please give him protection. Protect him physically. Give his mind a quietness and reduce the sound of the voices that he hears. Be his Great Physician and Comforter, Lord. I ask that you smile down from heaven and bless him with your grace and mercy today. We pray this in the name of Jesus Christ. Amen.

P13: Thank you, Chaplain.

Interpretation and Evaluation

Assessment of the Person

Wallace is a mannerly gentleman who is openly expressive with high-content communication. His large physical build and appearance could give off a spirit of intimidation and a don't-mess-with-me attitude. We, however, connected quickly, and I felt I had a good pastoral conversation with him.

Psychological Concerns

It was apparent to me that Wallace seeks affirmation and validation from others. He is talkative but he is unrelenting with talk about his faith and spiritual matters that are important to him—even if other people may be uncomfortable or unfamiliar with his topics. Does he have a psychological overlay? Does he indeed hear the voice of Satan or evil spirits/demons? I cannot judge and do not wish to do so.

Sociological/Cultural Concerns

I did not gain any information about Wallace's social support, living arrangements (whether he was homeless or not), or cultural background/ differences other than my own. We are both religious white males in the Bible Belt.

Theological Concerns

God and faith are very central to Wallace. He prays often and sees life through the lens of Scripture and God. I thought of the physical and personal hardships of Job who persevered the long trials as he relied upon his faith in God to help him persevere.

Personal Meaning

I found Wallace very interesting to speak with. I have had other encounters with people who had auditory hallucinations, which were primarily created by their own guilt and shame instead of having an organic mental problem (psychosis). I would have liked to have more time with Wallace for follow-up spiritual conversations to discover any underlying personal issues that were not dealt with yet.

Assessment of the Chaplain

I feel that this patient experienced me as a minister who gave him a listening ear and met him emotionally where he was at that time. I related the biblical parallel of Job's life of struggles and physical ailments that he endured by his strong faith in God. I feel that I offered Wallace understanding and empathy during our session.

Future Opportunities. What might you do differently if given the chance?

I would have like to have had more conversation about his life story and walk of faith. This might have shed more light upon his focus upon End Times (Antichrist) and being attacked by Satan.

Chaplain Keith Evans

To the Reader

- What are your initial thoughts about this encounter?
- Do you agree with or disagree with how the chaplain functioned?
- Would you have led the conversation differently or explored other areas of concern?
- Did the chaplain function professionally and with empathy and compassion?
- How was the spirituality of the individual assessed or not?
- Did the chaplain possess good skill sets in some areas and weak ones in others? What were those?
- After reading this verbatim, are you now aware of any skill set areas that you may need to improve upon?
- From the psychological perspective, what is the level of emotional awareness/expressivity? What are the major needs or conflicts (expressed and not expressed)? How do you perceive each person's self-image to be? Where is the power/control in this encounter (internal/external)? Did they relate to the chaplain as one-up, one-down, or as a peer?
- Were there any sociological and cultural concerns involved with this chaplain-family encounter? If so, what might they have been?
- Did you derive any personal meaning or connection from this verbatim?

VERBATIM 8

Fetal Demise[136]

Known Facts

Patient shared she was experiencing pain when visiting her husband in Mexico. She was twenty-eight weeks pregnant with no complications in her medical history. This was a regular routine visit to Mexico to visit her husband after he was deported nearly five years earlier. Patient was ambulanced to a hospital in southern Arizona where she mentioned doctors were communicating in secret and whispering about her condition. She was immediately flown to a larger medical center for more extensive evaluation and care. Patient said she only had pain and was unaware of seriousness of the situation. An emergency C-section was done because the baby had developed hydrocephalus in utero. The young baby girl lived thirty minutes before dying. Two other chaplain visits took place before my initial visit: one at time of death around two o'clock in the morning and the second after morning check-in. My visit was the third visit. I was paged around noon to offer support. This was my third fetal demise in three on-call shifts in a row.

---

[136] This verbatim was graciously contributed by SS Amar Atma Singh Khalsa LAC, MTCM. Chaplain Khalsa is an ordained minister of Sikh Dharma International and currently serves as a clinical chaplain at Banner University Medical Center in Phoenix, Arizona.

Chaplain Keith Evans

Description of the Patient and Setting

Preparing myself emotionally for the visit, I enter the closed-door room. I am overwhelmed by what I saw. The television is on, and chairs fill the room. Three young children huddle around a TV and eat junk food. Another young child was in the hospital bed with the mom, and three older women (one was the mother of the patient, and the other two were her sisters) are there. A toddler is rolling on the floor with a bottle in his mouth.

   I enter the room softly and gently since I am unsure of their grieving process. The baby who died had just been taken to another room. The nurse outside told me they wanted to take legal action against the doctors for not communicating or perhaps for not doing enough to save the baby since she was getting regular check-ups. A social worker is brought in to help understand the next steps if they are going to do an autopsy. They are prepared to receive the chaplain and began communicating right away, gratefully.

The Visit

I introduce myself as the chaplain. The patient nods and lets me know the baby had just been taken to another room because she was turning blue. It was difficult to continue looking at her deceased body. I offer my condolences for their loss and wait for what they need from me. The patient and her mom are busy with the social worker, so I patiently scan the room.

   I ask if I can sit in the empty chair and they oblige. I observe the mild chaos of the scene. My chair is next to the oldest child, George, who is fourteen. I turn and ask him how he's doing. I don't know what comes over me, but I start to engage the children in conversation. Lucas is twelve years old. He was in bed and joins the conversation.

C1: How are you feeling?
G1: I'm okay, I guess.
C2: Really? Okay?

Essential Chaplain Skill Sets

G2: No, not really. I'm actually pretty sad.
L2: Yeah, really sad.
C3: This is a very sad situation here. (Long pause.) What happened?
L3: (Shoulders shrug.) Our baby sister died. They just took her to the other room. She had a big
Head, and the doctor said she wasn't going to make it.
C4: Oh my. Did you see her?
L4: Yeah.
C5: How was that?
G5: (Shoulders shrug.) Sad.
C6: I bet. Have you seen anything like this before?
G6: No.
C7: Pretty scary to see the baby like that, huh?
L7: We don't know why she died.
C8: Why do you think?
L8: Because God took her.
C9: Do you believe in God?
L9: Yeah. (With a smile.)
C10: Heaven?
G10: Yeah, that's where she is. She's in a better place.
C11: (Echoes of grief-recovery class come through and the conditional training of rationalizing their experience that "she's in a better place." I believe that's what everyone has been saying and not what they really think themselves. I know not to go there and perpetuate this myth. I have their attention, and I engage toward their feelings.) Still sad though, huh?
G11: Yeah. (They both nod.)
C12: Even if she is in heaven, she's not here with you and your family. (Tears come down Lucas's face. George is pensive but does not express a lot outside.) Besides sadness, what else are you feeling?
G12: (Long pause.) Maybe anger.
C13: Okay. Anger. What are you angry about?
G13: Why did she have to die?
C14: So you're angry with God?

Chaplain Keith Evans

G14: (Confronted.) I don't know. (I can feel this stretched them because I believe they are mad at God, but they have been taught not to be.)

C15: Do you think God made a mistake?

L15: No. God doesn't make mistakes.

C16: Do you think God is punishing the family by taking her?

L16: No. God doesn't work that way.

C17: How does God work?

L17: God only does good. God decided this, but we don't know why.

C18: Yeah, it's really hard to know why this happened?

G19: Yeah, I don't really understand.

C20: Not knowing can get you pretty angry, huh?

G20: Yeah.

L20: I'm really sad.

C21: Are you feeling angry too?

L21: Yeah.

C22: This is a really hard place to be. Am I asking too many questions? Am I making you Uncomfortable? (They both take a moment.)

G22: No, it's okay.

C23: It feels good to talk about it, huh?

G23 Yeah.

C24: No one is really talking about this stuff, huh? (They nod.)

G24: Yeah, no one is saying anything. Everyone is sad, but they're not talking about it. Why is that?

C25: Right, it's so weird that everyone is maybe feeling the same way, but no one is expressing it. Feels kind of weird, like the way you're feeling is not okay. Do you feel you're supposed be different than what you're feeling?

G25: Yeah, it's confusing. All I want to do is talk about my baby sister, but it's weird that we're not saying anything about her.

L25: I just wish she was with us.

C26: You were excited to be with her?

L26: (He nods very quickly and very excitingly.)

C27: You were looking forward to a baby sister?

L28: Yes. Very much.

C29: So understandable to be sad and mad. (They both nod.) How much sad and how much mad? (I give them an example about what I mean.)

G29: I'm 50 percent mad and 50 percent sad.

C30: Anything else?

L30: Yeah, and I'm 20 percent worried.

C31: Worried?

L31: Yeah, I'm worried about my mom.

C32: Right. You're scared for her too?

L32: Yeah, we don't know if she's okay.

C33: You're taking good care of her being with her now?

L33: Yeah. We're giving her love.

C34: So, you are 50 percent mad, 50 percent sad, and 20 percent worried. Is that 120 percent?

L34: Yeah! (He says it so endearingly.)

C35: Well, I am sorry to hear about that. It is super tough to be feeling mad and sad and worried and then to have this other piece of being strong about it. (They both nod.) Tell me about God.

L35: What about God?

C36: Can you tell me about heaven? You said your baby sister is there. What do you think it's like?

L36: It's the best place.

C37: So this is in God's plan?

L37: I guess.

(During the conversation, I look over at the patient in the bed periodically. She has food on her tray and eats it often, which is a good sign. She looks pale, and I wonder about her health. She rests for much of the treatment. The kids are engaged with me, and I think it comforted her that she didn't have to attend to them. We went in and out of the threshold of vulnerability based on their attention spans, answering questions about my turban and my bracelet and my hair. The children are so intrigued by me. I answer simply, let them touch my turban, and engage them to build rapport so that we can talk comfortably about what they are feeling. They want to talk, but they don't know how to talk about what they were feeling. I also think they like the permission to feel what they are feeling. I approach this initial visit as spiritual listening and grief facilitation to help them cope effectively and verbalize their feelings. I support them in their process and work to empathize with their complex feelings. The initial visit was specific to the two oldest children in the room since the others were watching TV or catering to the young toddler touching everything in the room.)

Second Visit

I visit the family because of a referral from a social worker and to check in with them. I am surprised to know that the patient is still admitted. I check in with the nurse, and she explains that the patient developed hypertension. Since her blood pressure won't go down, they are keeping her here. She and her mom are the only ones inside.

C1: (Knocking on the door.) How's it going?
J1: Okay.
C2: You're still here?
J2: Yeah, the stress of my baby's death has given me high blood pressure.
C3: I'm so sorry to hear about that.
J3: Yes, it's been very hard.
C4: Understandable—it came all of a sudden. (She explains the story so that I am able to get a full picture of what is going on. She seems exhausted and is still slightly pale. I am worried about her health and wonder about any complications from the surgery. She is comfortable with me and opens up about her experience. She even lifts the gown to show me the staples. It surprised me that she exposes herself. Although she is wearing underwear, it still catches me off guard. Her surgery was substantial, starting up by her solar plexus and extending all the way down to her pubic bone. I ask if the kids will be coming back, and she shares they are on their way. I ask if it is

all right what we processed the other day, and she shares that they really enjoyed it and won't mind if I return.)

Third Visit

The room is less crowded but still as hectic. The older son sits closer to his mom in a large, comfortable chair. The younger one sat at the edge of the bed, and there was a chair for me. Another child is around ten years old, and he looks comfortable in a stroller.

C1: How's it going?
L1: Okay. We're glad you came back.
C2: Me too. I really enjoyed our talk the other day. How did you feel about it?
L2: It was nice to talk. My brother wanted to talk to you more.
C3: Oh yeah? What about?
L3: Just our feelings.
C4: I know. It's nice sometimes just to talk about how we are feeling. Still mad and sad today?
L4: I'm still sad, but I'm not as mad.
C5: Worried?
L5: No, not as worried. Mom is feeling better. She's leaving today if she can make her blood pressure go down.
C6: So less mad and still sad.
L6: Yeah—20 percent mad, and 60 percent sad.
C7: Okay, 80 percent today. That works.
L7: Yeah.
C8: George, between the time we talked and now, what has changed for you?
G9: We've had more time. We're feeling a little better, but we still miss her.
C9: Very understandable. It's such a sad thing that happened.
G9: We just don't understand why.
C10: It's hard to know reasons. Are you mad at God?
G10: (Reluctantly.) Yeah.

C11: Well, that is also understandable. It's hard to know God's point of view.
L11: It's really big, but we have faith.
C12: That's what everyone has been saying, huh?
G12: Yeah. (They both nod.)
C13: What does that mean? What does that mean to have faith?
L13: (Thinking.) God does everything, and God does good.
C14: Yeah? So how does this happen?
L14: He's teaching us.
C15: Okay, would you mind telling me more?
G15: In some ways I wonder why this couldn't happen to another family.
C16: Then they would feel like how you feel?
G16: Yeah. I don't want that. I'm okay.
C17: Sounds like you've really grown. Have you experienced a death in the family?
G17: No. This is our first one.
C18: And you saw her?
L18: Yeah, I took her picture. (He shows me the picture.) I like looking at it. Then I can remember her.
C19: Sounds beautiful.
L19: Yeah, all I want to do is talk about her.
C20: So tell me about her.
L20: Her face is glowing. Her eyes and mouth and nose didn't fully come out.
G20: She didn't stay in mom long enough.
L20: Yeah, her head was really big, but her body was really small.
C21: What about her hands and fingers?
L21: They were really small too—too small to even hold my one finger. (He talks with excitement.)
C22: Was it scary to see her?
G22: No. We wanted to see her.
C23: That takes a lot of courage.
L23: (He shrugs.) It's our baby sister. (He gets teary-eyed and wipes his eyes with his arm.)

C24: It's like that sometimes, huh, all the emotions? They're like the waves of the ocean.
L24: What do you mean?
C25: Well, have you been to California by the coast?
L25: Yeah?
C26: And you saw the ocean?
L26: Yeah?
C27: Did you notice sometimes that there are big waves and then small waves? And sometimes the ocean is really far up on the sand, and at other times, the beach looks so big?
L27: Yeah.
C28: Well, our feelings can be like that too. Sometimes a big wave of feeling comes out of nowhere. And sometimes you don't even have any feelings.
L28: Yeah, it sometimes comes in waves. (They both nod in excitement.)
C29: Exactly!
L29: Oh, yeah! Sometimes I'm sad, and then I'm mad, and then I get happy.
C30: Just like the waves in the ocean.

(The conversation goes substantially from there, and we use this as an opportunity to engage with the patient as well. She's in bed, and the two brothers share a seat. I introduce a game to them. I tune in to the different feelings they mention. I explain the game as if I am an alien who doesn't have a body or emotions or feelings. I am coming to learn about humans. I ask them to teach me about feelings. I introduce an emotion and ask them to close their minds and think about the baby girl who died and relate to that feeling. I ask them to pay attention to the sensation of the feelings in their bodies and where they feel it. It takes a few rounds, but they get it after a short time. The patient participates as well, which excites the kids. We go through happy, sad, mad, and love. It is profound, and they really enjoy it. They close their eyes and learn new ways of identifying their feelings. I approach the second and third visits to continue with empathy and really be in their shoes and support them in verbalizing their feelings and the grief process. I have a harder time with the mother than with the children. I credit them for being so insightful.)

Interpretation and Evaluation

Assessment

Since the mother was initially the focus of the visit, it was surprising that the children became the focus. Fetal demise has always been a personal struggle for me since I am not a woman, I am not a mother, and I have no children. I have to dig deep into the emotional space they may be feeling, and I recognize the injustice, the unfairness, and the questioning how and why the tragedy took place as an emotional basis for connection.

In actuality, children ministry is even more of a challenge for me. Children bring a certain truth to these situations and innocence to the emotional process. Adults tend to offer politeness when a visit doesn't go so well, but with children, there's a pure and unapologetic disengagement when an encounter doesn't serve them. I was afraid of being rejected by them. For that, the visit was challenging to me on both accounts.

I took the challenge. It would have been easy to leave when I noticed the patient was occupied with the social worker and her family. The disorderliness of the room was enough of an indicator that I did not want to be there, and that simple fact could have been enough of a justified excuse to leave. Something came over me, and I engaged the children, which proved to be fulfilling. I rose to the challenge to apply my pastoral authority and sat down and engaged the children. I faced my own fear in regard to children ministry. I felt my desire to empathize with the children, and helping them process was also fruitful for their growth. Since the mother was occupied with the details of her recovery, she wasn't able to care take of her children's emotional needs. The iPhones, video games, and TV were components that, at best, distracted them, leaving them emotionally vulnerable and unguided in a tragic event.

Psychological Concerns

After spending some time with them, I noticed how the children both took to the conversation about emotional processing. Lucas, being younger, had an innocent quality that was open and endearing. George was the oldest of all the children and had a particular guard up that kept me at arm's length. However, he also took to the conversation, which surprised me. I had to work harder with him to engage. I felt like I was fighting a cultural element of the male ego. He was the oldest, and his father was not totally present in his daily life. There were many children in the family, and I appreciated that his coming of age included him being "the man" of the house. I was cognizant to not displace him from an invisible throne and burden he felt called to hold or that was expected of him. I was also conscious that pain exists with that responsibility. I could sense that unanswered questions about life were presenting themselves, which was compounded by the circumstances of his life. He was old enough to reflect deeply, and he had a quiet, inquisitive nature. He was a deep thinker, and it was part of my purpose to engage him about his feelings more than Lucas because of Lucas's open and innocent nature.

Theological Reflection

According to Sikh theology, life is an arena to work out incomplete actions known as Karma. It's also an arena to promote Dharma, rightful actions. In other words, life isn't always as it seems and Scriptures guide us to the underlying truths and the essence of reality. Death is not what it seems in this context. Scripture says, "No one dies, and no one is capable of dying ... the soul does not perish; it is imperishable."

Raamkalee, Fifth Mehl

> The wind merges into the wind.
> The light blends into the light.
> The dust becomes one with the dust.

> What support is there for the one who is lamenting? ||1||
> Who has died? O, who has died?
> O, God, realized beings, meet together and consider this.
> What a wondrous thing has happened! ||1||Pause||
> No one knows what happens after death.
> The one who is lamenting will also arise and depart.
> Mortal beings are bound by the bonds of doubt and attachment.
> When life becomes a dream, the blind man babbles and grieves in vain. ||2||
> The Creator Lord created this creation.
> It comes and goes, subject to the will of the Infinite Lord.
> No one dies; no one is capable of dying.
> The soul does not perish; it is imperishable. ||3||
> That which is known, does not exist.
> I am a sacrifice to the one who knows this.
> Says Nanak, the Guru has dispelled my doubt.
> No one dies; no one comes or goes. ||4||10||

Sikh spirituality teaches us to meditate and worship God to gain the awareness of life beyond life. While death exists as a loss emotionally, spiritually, this life is not the only life. A conflict exists between the spiritual depth and the emotional process. In Sikh beliefs, there is life that exists before birth and life that exists after death. Grief is proportionally related to the awareness of the soul, to the eternal quality of our being. When we are not developed spiritually, loss is very difficult to manage because we experience the vast aloneness and emptiness of life without spirit. When the soul is engaged and a connection to spirituality is developed, the awareness of the true nature of reality dissolves the emotional burdens. It's not an intellectual understanding; it is an experiential one in which Sikhs gain perspective to this arena of life.

Shalok, Third Mehl

> Worship the Divine, Supreme Soul,
> With the intuitive peace and poise of the Guru.
> If the individual soul has faith in the Supreme Soul,
> Then it shall obtain realization within its own home.
> The soul becomes steady, and does not waver,
> By the natural inclination of the Guru's loving will.

With connection to the Supreme Soul, God, expanded awareness of our existence is expressed through intuitive understanding. Insights and deepened connections give space for the reality that underlies the common reality. This common reality based on our senses and perception is called *Maya* or illusion. With incomplete actions of our Karma, Maya plays a game that clouds over the essential nature of the divine within all. This is suffering. It's this oneness Sikhs aspire to—the essential nature of our true selves known as *Sat Nam*. Through meditation, we expand the senses and perception to tune into the underlying nature of things, commune with God, and live with bliss amid the difficult and challenging arenas of life.

I take these scriptures as support within this particular visit as emotional self-awareness, which is the first step toward a deeper awareness of the soul. Rather than avoiding or denying the real feelings of the children, I engaged them. I used my Sikh sense to engage the children in emotional and spiritual processing regarding the death of their baby sister. In this way, we expand beyond the moment or the loss without denying it. I'm guided by Scripture to find strength in the eternal quality of the soul. There are different stages of faith, but Sikhs believe there is a timeless wisdom within each represented as God. My goal was to tap that inner wisdom through emotional processing to give light to something spiritual.

> So many endure distress, deprivation, and constant abuse.
> Even these are Your Gifts, O Great Giver!

Chaplain Keith Evans

Assessment of the Chaplain

I understand that I cannot carry a person to the spirituality we strive to attain as Sikhs. I also understand that the development of emotional self-awareness is a necessary step for emotional and spiritual well-being. I felt the children stirring with emotional distress and the death of their baby sister. While the mother was engaged, I took advantage of the opportunity to be with the children. The second visit with the children proved to be helpful for them. They inquired and requested support. We engaged with the mother as well, helping to deepen faith, name feelings, and verbalize grief regarding the death. We played it as a game for emotional development, which reflected the Scripture that gifts may be present even in distress.

Future Opportunities

Do more referrals or follow-up meetings need to be arranged by the chaplains? What more should be planned or could have been done differently?

To the Reader

- What are your initial thoughts about this encounter?
- Do you agree with or disagree with how the chaplain functioned?
- Would you have led the conversation differently or explored other areas of concern?
- Did the chaplain function professionally and with empathy and compassion?
- How was the spirituality of the individual assessed or not?
- Did the chaplain possess good skill sets in some areas and weak ones in others? What were those?
- After reading this verbatim, are you now aware of any skill set areas that you may need to improve upon?
- From the psychological perspective, what is the level of emotional awareness/expressivity? What are the major needs

or conflicts (expressed and not expressed)? How do you perceive each person's self-image to be? Where is the power/control in this encounter (internal/external)? Did they relate to the chaplain as one up, one down, or as a peer?
- Were there any sociological and cultural concerns involved with this chaplain-family encounter? If so, what might they have been?
- Did you derive any personal meaning or connection from this verbatim?

BIBLIOGRAPHY

Anandarajah, Gowri. "The 3 H and BMEST Models for Spirituality in Multicultural Whole-Person Medicine." *Annals of Family Medicine* 6, no. 5 (2008): 448–458.

Anandarajah, Gowri, and Ellen Hight. "Spirituality and Medical Practice: Using the HOPE Questions as a Practical Tool for Spiritual Assessment." *Am Fam Physician* 63, no. 1 (January 1, 2001): 81–89.

Ashmos, Donde P., and Dennis Duchon. "Spirituality at Work. A Conceptualization and Measure." *Journal of Management Inquiry* 9, no. 2 (2000): 134–145.

Ashton, John and Whyte, Tom. *The Quest for Paradise*. San Francisco: HarperCollins, 2001.

Balboni, Tracy, et al. "Support of Cancer Patient's Spiritual Needs and Associations with Medical Care Costs at the End of Life" *Cancer* 117 (2011): 5383–5391. http://www.ncbi.nlm.nih.gov/pmc/articles/PMC3177963

Barrett, D. *World Christian Encyclopedia,* (2nd ed.). New York: Oxford, 2001.

Benjaminson, Chana. "The Seder Service in a Nutshell." www.Chabad.org.

Benner, David B. *Care of Souls: Revisioning Christian Nurture and Counsel*. Grand Rapids: Baker Books, 1998.

Bonhoeffer, Dietrich. *Ethics*. New York: Macmillan Publishing Company, 1955.

Brown, Brene'. *The Gifts of Imperfection*. Center City: Hazelden, 2010.

Brown, Brene'. *I Thought It was Just Me (But it isn't)* New York: Gotham Books, 2007.

Brown, Brene'. *Daring Greatly: How the Courage to Be Vulnerable Transforms the Way We Live, Love, Parent, and Lead.* New York: Gotham Books, 2012.

Clinebell, Howard. Basic Types of Pastoral Care and Counseling: Resources for the Ministry of Healing and Growth. Nashville: Abingdon Press, 1984.

"Common Qualifications and Competencies for Professional Chaplains" Association of Professional Chaplains. Accessed on May 9, 2017. www.professionalchaplains.org

Covey, Stephen R. *The 7 Habits of Highly Effective People, Signature Edition 4.0.* Salt Lake City: Franklin Covey, date not listed.

Coward, Harold (ed.). *Life after Death in World Religions.* Maryknoll, NY: Orbis Books, 1997.

Elass, Mateen. "Four Jihads" *Christianity Today* (2002). Accessed October 7, 2014. www.haventoday.org/dr-mateen-elass-four-jihads-gd-125.html

Elkins, David N., L. James Hedstrom, Lori L. Hughes, J. Andrew Leaf and Cheryl Saunders, "Toward a Humanistic-Phenomenological Spirituality: Definition, Description, and measurement" *Journal of Humanistic Psychology* 28, no. 5 (1988): 7.

Erickson, Millard J. *Christian Theology,* 2nd ed. Grand Rapids: Baker Academic, 1998.

Everly Jr., George S. Pastoral Crisis Intervention: Course Workbook. Ellicott City, MD: Chevron Press, 2002.

Fairholm, Gilbert. *Capturing the Heart of Leadership: Spirituality and Community in the New American Workplace.* Westport: Praeger Publishers, 1997. Accessed July 29, 2014. http://books.google.com.

Fetzer Institute. "Multidimensional measurement of religiousness/spirituality for use in health research." Bethesda: Fetzer Institute, *National Institute of Aging* (1999): 1–95.

Fitchett, George. *Assessing Spiritual Needs: A Guide for Caregivers.* Minneapolis: Augsburg Fortress, 1993.

Flannelly, Kevin J., et al. "A National Study of Chaplaincy Services and End of Life Outcomes" *BMC Palliative Care* 11, no. 10 (2012): 1, accessed September 1, 2013, http://biomedcentral.com/1472-684x/11/10.

Fowler, James W. *Stages of Faith: The Psychology of Human Development and the Quest for Meaning*, New York, NY: Harper Collins Publishers, 1981.

Friedman, Carey A. *Spiritual Survival for Law Enforcement.* NJ: Compass Books, 2015.

Fry, Louis W., and Yochanan Altman. *Spiritual Leadership in Action: The CEL Story, Achieving Extraordinary Results through Ordinary People.* Charlotte: Information Age Publishing, Inc. 2013.

Fry, Louis W., and Melissa Sadler Nisiewicz. *Maximizing the Triple Bottom Line through Spiritual Leadership.* Stanford: Stanford Business Books, 2013. Kindle eBook Location 1096–1116.

Giacalone, Robert A., Carole J. Jurkiewicz, and Louis W. Fry. "From Advocacy to Science: The Next Steps in Workplace Spirituality Research" In *Handbook of the Psychology of Religion and Spirituality,* eds. Raymond F. Paloutzian and Crystal L. Park. New York: Guilford Publications, 2005, 521.

Gilmartin, Kevin. *Emotional Survival for Law Enforcement.* E-S Press, 2002.

Gokulmuthu Narayanaswamy, *Tenets of Hinduism*, (2013), https://www.scribd.com/doc/223463442/tenets-of-Hinduism-Gokulmuthu-Narayanaswamy.

Govinda, Lama Anagarika. *Foundations of Tibetan Mysticism.* Boston: Weiser Books, 1969.

Gray, Jason D. "Buddhist Views of the Afterlife." The Immortality Project of University of California at Riverside. www.sptimmortalityproject.com

Green, Matthew. *The Message of Matthew.* The Bible Speaks Today Commentary Series, Downers Grove, IL: Inter-Varsity Press, 2000.

Gregory, Joel C. *Gregory's Sermon Synopses: 200 Expanded Summaries.* Nashville: Broadman Press, 1991.

Grudem, Wayne. *Systematic Theology: An Introduction to Biblical Doctrine.* Grand Rapids: Zondervan, 1994.

Guillory, William A. *Spirituality in the Workplace: A Guide for Adapting to the Chaotically Changing Workplace.* Salt Lake City: Innovations International Inc. Publishing, 1997.

Gyatso, Geshe Kelsang. *Modern Buddhism: The Path of Compassion and Wisdom, Vol. 2: Tantra.* Glen Spey, NY: Tharpa Publications, 2011.

Healthcare Chaplaincy. "Handbook of Patient's Spiritual and Cultural Values for Health Care Professionals" HealthCare Chaplaincy Network. New York, 2013.

Hill, Clara E. *Helping Skills: Facilitating, Exploration, Insight, and Action.* Washington: American Psychological Association.

Holloway, A.G. *Buddhism: The Buddhists Way of Knowing Buddha.* Amazon Kindle e-book, 2014.

Iserson, Kenneth V. *Pocket Protocols: Notifying Survivors about Sudden, Unexpected Deaths.* Tucson: Galen Press, Ltd, 1999.

Josephus, Flavius. *The Complete Works of Flavuis Josephus.* 2014, e-book.

Kinjerski, Val, and Berna J. Skrypnek. "Measuring the Intangible: Development of the Spirit at Work Scale" in *Best Paper Proceedings of the Sixty-fifth Annual Meeting of the Academy of Management* (CD). Editor M. Weaver. (2006): A1–A6.

Kinjerski, Val, and Berna J. Skrypnek. "A Human Ecological Model of Spirit at Work." *Journal of Management, Spirituality & Religion* 3, no. 3 (2006): 232–239.

Koenig, Harold G., George R. Parkerson, Jr. and Keith G. Meador, "Religion Index for Psychiatric Research" *The American Journal of Psychiatry* 154, no 6 (June 1997): 885–886. Accessed October 4, 2014. www.psychnet.apa.org.

Koenig, Harold G. *Spirituality and Health Research: Methods, Measurements, Statistics and Resources.* West Conshohocken: Templeton Press, 2011.

Koenig, Harold G., Dana E. King, and Verna Benner Carson, *Handbook of Spirituality and Health*, 2nd edition. Oxford: Oxford University Press, 2012.

LaRocca-Pitts, Mark. "FACT: Taking a spiritual history in a clinical setting" *Journal of Health Care Chaplaincy* 15, no 1 (2009):1–12.

Lindbeck, George A. *The Nature of Doctrine: Religion and Theology in a Postliberal Age.* Philadelphia: Westminster, 1984.

Lynn, Monty L., Michael J. Naughton, and Steve VanderVeen. "Faith at Work Scale (FWS): Justification, Development, and Validation of a Measure of Judaeo-Christian Religion in the Workplace." *Journal of Business Ethics* 85, no. 2 (2009): 227–243.

Malphurs, Aubrey. A New Kind of Church: Understanding Models of Ministry for the 21st Century. Grand Rapids, MI: Baker Books, 2007.

Marques, Joan, Satinder Dhiman and Richard King. *Spirituality in the Workplace: What It Is, Why It Matters, How To Make It Work For You.* Fawnskin: Personhood Press, 2007.

Maugans, TA. "The SPIRITual history" *Arch Fam Med* 5, Issue 1 (1996):11–16.

McSherry, Wilford and Linda Ross. *Spiritual Assessment in Healthcare Practice.* London: M & K Publishing, 2010.

Miller, Chaim. *Torah: The Five Books of Moses with Complete Haftarah Cycle.* Brooklyn: Lifestyle Books, 2011.

Miller, David W. *God at Work: The History and Promise of the Faith at Work Movement.* Oxford: Oxford University Press, 2007.

Miller, David W. "The Faith at Work Movement: It's Growth, Dynamics and Future," Ph.D. diss., Princeton University, 2003.

Miller, David W., and Timothy Ewest. "The Integration Box (TIB): An Individual and Institutional Faith, Religion, and Spirituality at Work Assessment Tool" www.princeton.edu.

Narayanaswamy, Gokulmuthu, *Tenets of Hinduism,* Publisher unknown, 2013. Accessed October 7, 2014. https://scribd.com/doc/223563442/Tenets-of-Hinduism-Gokulmuthu-Narayanaswamy.

Nasr, Seyyed Hossein, ed. *Islamic Spirituality: Foundations,* Volume 19 of *World Spirituality: An Encyclopedic History of the Religious Quest.* New York: Crossroad Publishing, 1997.

Nasr, Seyyed Hossein, ed. *Islamic Spirituality: Manifestations,* Volume 20 of *World Spirituality: An Encyclopedic History of the Religious Quest.* New York: Crossroad Publishing, 1997.

Neal, Judith A. "Spirituality in the Workplace." accessed May 22, 2014, http://judineal.com/pages/pubs/academic1.htm#spirit.

Paloutzian, Raymond F., and C. W. Ellison. "Loneliness, spiritual well-being and quality of life." In *Loneliness: A Sourcebook of Current Theory, Research and Therapy.* Editors L. A. Peplau and D. Perlman. New York: Wiley (1982): 224–237.

Pandey, Ashish, Rajen K. Gupta and A. P. Arora. "Spiritual Climate of Business Organizations and Its Impact on Customer Experience." *Journal of Business Ethics* 88, no. 2 (2009): 313–332.

Pargament, Kenneth I. *The Psychology of Religion and Coping: Theory, Research, Practice.* New York: Guilford Press, 1997.

Perkins, Tasi. "Beyond Jacques Derrida and George Lindbeck: Toward a Particularity-Based Approach to Interreligious Communication," *Journal of Ecumenical Studies* (June 2013) 48:3, pages unknown. http://www.thefreelibrary.com (accessed March 21, 2014).

Petchsawanga, Pawinee, and Dennis Duchon. "Workplace Spirituality, Meditation, and Work Performance." *Journal of Management, Spirituality and Religion* 9, no. 2 (June 2012): 190.

Phillips, W. Gary, William E. Brown and John Stonestreet. *Making Sense of Your World: A Biblical Worldview.* Salem, WI: Sheffield Publishing, 2008.

Pruitt, Richard A. "Rethinking Postliberal Theology: Comparing and Contrasting Lindbeck and Vanhoozer," *Evangelical Review of Theology* 36 (2012):2, 161–175.

Puchalski, Christina, and A. L. Romer "Taking a spiritual history allows clinicians to understand patients more fully" *J Pall Med*, 3 (2000):129–137.

Puchalski, Christina M., Robert Vitillo, Sharon K. Hull and Nancy Reller. "Improving the Spiritual Dimension of Whole Person Care: Reaching National and International Consensus." *Journal of Palliative Medicine* 17, no. 6, (2014): 642, accessed June 22, 2014, http://online.liebertpub.com.

Robinson, Douglas Edward. "Pastoral Care: A New Model For Assessing the Spiritual Needs of Hospitalized Patients." DMin dissertation. Liberty Baptist Theological Seminary, (August 2012): 111–112. www.digitalcommons.liberty.edu

Saint-Laurent, George E. *Spirituality and World Religions: A Comparative Introduction*. Mountain View: Mayfield Publishing Co, 2000.

Sire, James W. *The Universe Next Door: A Basic Worldview Catalog*. Fifth Ed. Downers Grove, IL: InterVarsity Press, 2009.

Stoll, Ruth. *Guidelines for Spiritual Assessment*, 1979; also in McSherry, W., and Linda Ross. *Spiritual Assessment in Healthcare Practice*. London: M & K Publishing, 2010.

Sunshine, Glenn, *Portals: Entering your Neighbor's World*. Newington, CT: Every Square Inch Publishing, 2012.

Tzortis, Hamza Andreas. "What is Islamic Spirituality?" www.hamzatzortis.com.

V., Jayaram. "Death and Afterlife in Hinduism" and Afterlife in Hinduism." www.hinduwebsite.com

VandeCreek, Larry, and Laurel Burton. *Professional Chaplaincy: Its role and Importance in Healthcare*. Schaumburg, IL: Association of Professional Chaplains, 2001; also VandeCreek, Larry, and Laurel Burton, eds. "Professional Chaplaincy: Its Role and Importance in Healthcare." *The Journal of Pastoral Care* 55, no. 1 (Spring 2001): 82.

Warren, Rick. *The Purpose Driven Church: Growth Without Compromising Your Message & Mission*, Grand Rapids, MI: Harper Collins Publishers, 1995.

Washington Ethical Society, "What is humanistic spirituality?" www.ethicalsociety.org.

Wendling, Rich, and Daniel Shayesteh, "Islam's View of Sin and Salvation: Reaching Muslims, Part 2." www.answersingenesis.org

Wilson, M. R. "Judaism" in *Evangelical Dictionary of Theology* 2nd ed., ed. Walter A. Elwell. Grand Rapids: Baker Academic, 2001.

Yoshinori, Takeuchi, ed. *Buddhist Spirituality: Indian, Southeast Asian, Tibetan, Early Chinese* Volume 8 of *World Spirituality: An Encyclopedic History of the Religious Quest*. New York: Crossroad Publishing, 1997.

ABOUT THE AUTHOR

Rev. Dr. Keith A. Evans, DC, DMin
Board-Certified Chaplain

Evans is an ordained Christian minister and a board-certified professional chaplain. Evans has served in a trauma hospital and as a law enforcement chaplain. Prior to his calling into ministry, Evans worked for two decades in chiropractic health care. He developed many of his learned skill sets through working with patients in acute and chronic physical pain and through counseling individuals dealing with disabling life situations.

Evans holds a master's of divinity (MDiv) degree with chaplaincy concentration from Liberty University and a doctor of ministry (DMin) in theology and pastoral counseling degree from Temple Baptist Seminary at Piedmont International University. He also has a professional doctorate degree in chiropractic (DC) from Parker College of Chiropractic as well as BA and MA degrees in biblical counseling from Trinity College of the Bible and Theological Seminary. Evans is a board-certified clinical chaplain with the Association of Professional Chaplains. He also has earned specialty certificates in palliative care chaplaincy and integrative chaplaincy.

Evans currently serves as the senior manager of Spiritual Care Services at Banner Thunderbird Medical Center in Glendale, Arizona. He is also an adjunct faculty member for Grand Canyon University's College of Theology, teaching courses on spiritual and ethical decision making in health care. Evans is a commissioned Colson Fellow with the Colson Center for Christian Worldview.

Made in the USA
Middletown, DE
05 December 2021